VANGUARD SERIES

EDITOR: MARTIN WINDROW

ARMOUR OF THE KOREAN WAR 1950-53

Text by SIMON DUNSTAN

Colour plates by TERRY HADLER

D1716250

OSPREY PUBLISHING LONDON

Published in 1982 by
Osprey Publishing, Elms Court, Chapel Way,
Botley, Oxford OX2 9LP, United Kingdom.
© Copyright 1982 Osprey Publishing Ltd

Reprinted 1984, 1985 (twice), 1989
Special Reprint 2001

ISBN 0 85045 428 X

Filmset in Great Britain
Printed in China through World Print Ltd

Dedication To Rebecca

Front cover illustration A Sherman M4A3 (76)
W HVSS of Co. 'C', 89th Tank Bn., US 2nd Infantry
Division, photographed north of the Han River, March
1951. The white star was normally carried well forward
on the hull side; some tanks of the unit carried
individual names in white block or script roughly
central on the hull side.

Invasion from the North

In the early morning of Sunday 25 June 1950 the North Korean People's Army (NKPA) swept across the 38th Parallel at eleven separate points to invade the Republic of Korea (ROK). With many battle-hardened veterans who had fought in the Chinese Communist armies against Chiang Kai-Shek, the well-trained NKPA comprised seven infantry divisions and units of the Border Constabulary supported by heavy artillery, the 105th Armoured Brigade and an effective air force, with three divisions in reserve.

The South Korean Army was ill-equipped to meet such an onslaught. It possessed neither heavy artillery, air support nor armour, except for the cavalry regiment of the Capital Division in Seoul, equipped with 27 M8 armoured cars for ceremonial duties and the protection of the presidential palace.

Lacking any anti-tank weapons other than ineffective 37mm anti-tank guns and obsolescent 2.36in. bazookas, the South Koreans resisted the invaders as best they could, improvising anti-tank weapons from satchel-charges and hand grenades. Some volunteers adopted suicide tactics, hurling themselves and the high explosives they carried under the bellies of T-34s. Others clambered on to enemy tanks in a desperate effort to lever open

At the forefront of the North Korean invasion in June 1950 were 120 T-34/85s of 105th Armoured Brigade. A further 30, manned by personnel of the tank training unit at Sadong, supported the NKPA 7th Div. on the east-central front in the attack against Inje. Demoralised by their lack of modern anti-tank weapons, the South Korean army invariably fled when attacked by tanks. A large measure of the North Korean success in the early battles of the war was due to the T-34, belying the assumption of US military advisers that armour could not be employed effectively in such a mountainous country. (ROK Army)

their hatches and drop grenades inside. A few tanks were destroyed in this way, but volunteers soon became scarce.

The main thrust of the Communist offensive was directed down the Uijongbu Corridor towards the South Korean capital Seoul, 50 miles to the south—the traditional invasion route from the north since the time of the Golden Horde. In the face of such overwhelming superiority the ROK forces retreated, and President Syngman Rhee, the autocratic leader of South Korea, appealed to the United Nations for assistance. The United States immediately came to South Korea's aid with air and naval forces. On 29 June President Truman authorised General of the Army Douglas MacArthur, who had been named Commander in Chief, United Nations Command, to commit US ground forces in Korea.

The United States was hardly in a condition to wage war in the summer of 1950. Due to popular sentiment against a large standing military

3

M26 Pershing of the Provisional Tank Platoon, the first American medium tank unit in Korea, photographed during gunnery training near Taegu, 22 July 1950. In the background are examples of the M24 Chaffee light tanks and M8 Greyhound armoured cars that equipped reconnaissance companies of US infantry divisions. Neither of these vehicles proved particularly successful in Korea, being totally outclassed by the T-34/85. (US Army SC 343812)

establishment and the drastic reductions in defence expenditure in the years since 1945, the Army was a shadow of its wartime strength. The only available units in the Far East were on occupation duties in Japan, where soldiering had taken second place to the less exacting tasks of civil administration and the delights of Tokyo's Ginza district. The 7th, 24th and 25th Infantry Divisions and 1st Cavalry Division (organised as infantry) of the US Eighth Army in Japan were all under strength. These formations had assigned to them the 77th, 78th, 79th and 71st Tank Battalions respectively, but only one company ('A') of each battalion had been activated and then only with M24 Chaffee light tanks. It was feared that heavier tanks would damage Japanese roads and bridges.

General MacArthur immediately despatched elements of 1st Bn., 21st Infantry Regt. of 24th Infantry Div., under the command of Lt. Col. Charles B. Smith, by air to the South Korean port of Pusan. With the remainder of the division following by sea, Task Force Smith moved north and made contact with the enemy in the vicinity of Osan on 5 July.

Early that morning Smith's diminutive and lightly armed force detected a column of T-34/85s advancing through the rain and mist. Undeterred by HE fire or by direct hits from Smith's two recoilless-rifles, the enemy tanks plunged into the heart of the position, firing erratically. The two leading tanks were knocked out by 105mm howitzer HEAT rounds, but the Americans had only six of these, and HE shells simply bounced off the enemy armour. Twenty-two rockets from 2.36in. bazookas were fired at point-blank range but without appreciable effect. Thirty-three T-34s of 107th Armoured Regiment took part in this attack—only four were immobilised. After seven gruelling hours Task Force Smith was forced to withdraw.

The failure of American anti-tank weapons in this action and the poor performance of the M24 light tanks when first committed at Chonui on 10 July only added to the myth of the T-34's invincibility. Morale suffered accordingly. Despite the appearance of the effective 3.5in. bazooka, airlifted from the United States, at the battle of Taejon, and repeated strikes from the air, North Korean armoured thrusts advanced almost unchecked. With the fall of Taejon on 20 July UN forces fell back, trading space for time to reinforce the perimeter around Pusan with units arriving from America. High on the list of priorities was a demand for tanks. The Department of the Army reacted swiftly and on 10 July three tank battalions were put on alert for Korea. These were the 6th (M46 Patton), 70th (M26 Pershing and M4A3 Sherman) and 73rd (M26 Pershing) Battalions. The 70th and 73rd were the school troop battalions of the Armor School at Fort Knox and of the Infantry School at Fort Benning respectively. The 6th was an organic battalion of 2nd Armoured Division. They were the only armoured formations in the United States ready for immediate combat. Their transports sailed from San Francisco on 23 July and arrived at Pusan on 7 August.

While these movements were taking place Eighth Army activated the 8072nd Medium Tank Bn. in Japan. This unit received 54 rebuilt M4A3 Shermans. These were mostly late-production models with Horizontal Volute Spring Suspension (HVSS) and 76mm guns, salvaged from the Pacific islands after the Second World War and refurbished in Japan. Company 'A' arrived in Korea on 31 July and went into battle two days later.

However, these Shermans were not the first American medium tanks to see action in Korea.

On the fourth day of the war three M26 Pershings were discovered at Tokyo Ordnance Depot. All were in poor condition, requiring extensive repairs, including rebuilt engines. Work began immediately and was completed by 13 July. The three Pershings were then shipped to Pusan, where they arrived three days later. With them were 1st Lt. Samuel R. Fowler and 14 enlisted men drawn from 'A' Co., 77th Tank Bn. who, having trained on M24 Chaffees, now had to familiarise themselves with the heavier M26 very rapidly. During training and gunnery practice near Taegu it became apparent that the rebuilt engines were cause for grave concern. Standard-issue fanbelts had been unavailable in Japan and those made locally were either too long or too short. The latter would not fit at all and the former slipped so badly that the engines overheated.

Nevertheless the need for tanks to stem the enemy advance on Pusan was so insistent that these vehicles were sent by rail to Chinju on 28 July. They were still there, waiting for new fanbelts, when on 31 July the NKPA 6th Div. broke into the town. After accounting for a number of the enemy with their machine guns the three Pershings withdrew eastwards, only to be halted by a blown

M19 Gun Motor Carriage of 82nd AAA AW Battalion (SP) of 2nd Infantry Div. overlooking the Naktong River—the last natural barrier protecting the western approaches to Pusan—on 6 September 1950. Based on the chassis of the M24 Light Tank, the M19 was originally dubbed 'flak-wagon', but in Korea it earned the dubious title of 'rolling coffin' as the open fighting-compartment proved to be a convenient receptacle for enemy grenades. As there was no enemy air ground-attack activity self-propelled AA vehicles were successfully employed in an infantry support rôle. Note the sandbags lashed to the gunshield to augment the thin armour, and spare 40mm gun barrels across the engine decks. (US Army SC 348000)

bridge. When the crewmen attempted to destroy their tanks with grenades they came under fire, and only one Pershing managed to escape the way it had come. Shortly afterwards the overheated engine stalled and refused to start again. The only three medium tanks in Korea had been lost.

The Pusan Perimeter

Among the units assigned to Korea after the outbreak of the war was 1st Marine Division. General MacArthur had intended that this formation undertake its established rôle as an amphibious assault force somewhere on the Korean peninsula, in order to sever the enemy's lines of communication—but such was the need for American ground troops to bolster the ever-shrinking

Inchon, 15 September 1950: LCU (Landing Craft Utility) carrying M26s of 3 Ptn., Co. 'A', 1st Marine Tank Bn., churns towards Wolmi-Do island against a backdrop of smoke and flame as naval guns and USMC aircraft batter the port of Inchon.
(Soldier)

perimeter around Pusan that all available troops had to be committed immediately. Accordingly the advance element of the division, 1st Provisional Marine Brigade, was diverted from its destination of Kobe in Japan to Korea. Such was the haste of mobilisation that in most instances there was insufficient time even for weapons training. Company 'A' of 1st Marine Tank Bn. had been accustomed to the M4A3 Sherman—activated on 7 July for service with the Brigade, the unit was equipped with M26 Pershings. Only one day of training was achieved on the new vehicles, with each crew limited to firing two rounds of main armament ammunition, before sailing. The 90mm guns were not fired again until taken into combat in Korea.

The brigade placed heavy reliance on its tanks to counter the success of North Korean armour, and were confident that their M26s were more than a match for the T-34/85. On 12 July Company 'A', 1st Marine Tank Bn., and elements of 1st Marine Amphibian Tractor Bn. sailed from San Diego on board the LSDs (Landing Ship Dock) *Fort Marrion* and *Gunston Hall*. On the following day the well deck of the *Fort Marrion* flooded, with water rising five feet deep among the M26s. An hour passed before the ship was pumped dry, but salt water had damaged 14 of the tanks as well as 300 main armament rounds (then in critically short supply) and 5,000 rounds of .30 calibre. When

news of the flood damage reached Brigade Headquarters at San Diego frantic efforts were made to find replacement tanks and ammunition. Fortunately it was possible to repair 12 of the tanks on board the *Fort Marrion*, while the two remaining M26s required only replacement parts and were repaired within 72 hours of disembarkation.

On arrival the Pershings were immediately committed to combat during the Sachon counter-offensive in the customary Marine tank rôle of infantry support; but the first significant tank engagement occurred during the battle of the Naktong Bulge, when 1st Marine Provisional Bde., acting under operational control of 24th Infantry Div., strove to destroy the bridgehead of the NKPA 4th Div. over the Naktong River.

Throughout 17 August the M26s of 3 Platoon, 'Able' Company Tanks supported the attack of 2/5 Marines (2nd Bn., 5th Marine Regt.) against Hill 102 at the northern end of Obong-Ni ridge. Commanded by 2nd Lt. Granville Sweet, the tanks engaged enemy heavy weapons along the crest, and by late afternoon had destroyed at least 12 anti-tank guns and several automatic weapons. After the objective had been seized the platoon withdrew to the east of Observation Hill for replenishment.

As dusk fell, Marines on Hill 102 observed four T-34/85s (of 107th Armoured Regt.) approaching the brigade lines along the road to the west. Patrolling F4U Corsairs of MAG-33 attacked the column, destroying the fourth tank and dispersing the accompanying infantry. An ambush of bazookas and recoilless-rifles was hastily prepared for the remaining three tanks, while the Pershings of 3 Ptn.—which were still refuelling and replenishing their ammunition—were called forward. As the first T-34 rounded the bend between Observation Hill and Hill 125 it was hit by bazooka and recoilless-rifle fire and burst into flames. With its guns firing wildly, the enemy tank continued round the corner and came face to face with a Pershing. The T-34 was hit twice by 90mm gunfire and exploded. The second T-34 was struck in the fuel tank by a bazooka round and then by a fusillade of recoilless-rifle fire. It lurched to a halt beside the blazing remains of the first tank, but continued to fire its weapons haphazardly. By this time a second M26 had manoeuvred in beside the other on the narrow road, and the two Pershings blasted the T-34 with 13 rounds before it too exploded. The third T-34 suffered a similar fate under the combined fire of Marine tanks, bazookas and recoilless-rifles. The myth of the T-34's invincibility had been shattered. Not only Corsairs and Pershings but also every organic Marine infantry weapon had been instrumental in this defeat of Communist armour.

Throughout August the battle raged around the Pusan perimeter while reinforcements poured in from America, as well as contingents from other UN armies, including 27th British Commonwealth Infantry Brigade. During the month five US tank battalions landed in Korea. The tanks in the battalions were almost equally divided between Pershings and Shermans, except for 6th Tank Bn., which was equipped with M46 Pattons. Each battalion had on average 69 tanks. The tank units in Korea in August were: 6th, 70th, 72nd, 73rd and 89th Tank Bns. (the 8072nd had been redesignated the 89th Medium Tank Bn. on 7 August) plus elements of 71st and 77th Tank Bns.

from Japan; the 9th and 38th regimental tank companies of 2nd Infantry Div.; the regimental tank company of 5th Regimental Combat Team; Company 'A', 1st Marine Tank Bn. and approximately 30 M24 Chaffees of the Reconnaissance Companies of 2nd, 24th and 25th Infantry Divs. and 1st Cavalry Division. In all there were more than 400 American medium tanks within the Pusan pocket by the end of the month, outnumbering the enemy by at least four to one. The North Koreans had received some reinforcements including 80 T-34/85s which equipped two new tanks units, the 16th and 17th Armoured Brigades. Others were delivered to the 105th Armoured Division, but aerial action destroyed many new tanks before they could reach the battle zone.

After the capture of Inchon the Marines thrust inland towards Seoul and the strategic airfield at Kimpo. Here, an M26 of Co. 'B', 1st Marine Tank Bn., accompanied by LVT-3s of 1st Marine Amphibian Tractor Bn., advances on Kimpo with 3/5 Marines; 17 September 1950. (US Army SC 349015)

The Inchon Landings

From the very outset of the war General MacArthur had determined on an amphibious operation aimed at enveloping the over-extended enemy from the rear. He selected Inchon as the beach-head—it being the closest port to Seoul and the hub of communications into South Korea. Hydrographic conditions in the restricted waterway of Inchon made the plan a hazardous one, but MacArthur overrode the heated protests of many senior officers, and X Corps was activated in Japan with 1st Marine and 7th Infantry Divs. together with four battalions of ROK Marines.

The necessary logistical build-up was effected in a remarkably short time and the invasion fleet arrived off Inchon in the early hours of 15 September. As aircraft and naval guns pounded the harbour defences, 3/5 Marines landed at 0630 on Wolmi-Do, an island linked by a causeway to the mainland. It was essential that Wolmi-Do be captured prior to the main assaults as its guns dominated both Inchon and the landing beaches to north and south. At 0646 three LCUs comprising the third wave broached on Green Beach to disgorge a detachment of Company 'A', 1st Marine Tank Battalion. Ten tanks were landed—six M26s, one M4A3 flamethrower, two

One of the few weapons effective against North Korean armour in the early battles was napalm—a widely used but incorrect term for jellied gasoline—dropped by ground-attack aircraft. In the first two years of the war the US Air Force claimed the destruction of 1,134 AFVs, as against 121 destroyed by ground weapons. Not only is the ratio erroneous, but the total claimed is more than the number of AFVs employed by the Communists throughout the war!

(Soldier)

M4A3 tankdozers and one M32 TRV. Within minutes the tanks were in action when Marines of 'Item' Company were attacked with grenades from a line of enemy emplacements dug into a low cliff along the shoreline facing Inchon. When called upon to surrender the North Koreans responded with another flurry of grenades and 'Item' Company commander signalled up the tanks. With Pershings and riflemen giving covering fire a tankdozer rumbled forward, gathering earth and rubble with its blade, and entombed the enemy in their dug-outs. By noon Wolmi-Do was captured, and gradually the extraordinary invasion tide receded revealing the treacherous mudflats all around. Through the early afternoon an oppressive silence settled over the area as 3/5 Marines, fearful of a counter-attack across the causeway or mudflats, waited for the evening tide when the major assaults against Inchon would begin. However, the enemy made only one foray against Wolmi-Do, when an armoured car sped along the causeway. An alert M26 tracked the speeding vehicle for a few seconds and then fired. The BA-64 disintegrated under the impact of a single round.

At 1730 2/5 Marines clambered over the seawall at Red Beach, with the Pershings on Wolmi-Do giving covering fire. At the same time 1st Marines mounted in LVTs of 1st Amphibian Tractor Bn. landed on Blue Beach. Under the supporting fire of LVT(A)5s of 56th Amphibious Tank and Tractor Bn., the Marines advanced inland against sporadic resistance. Immediately following the assault troops eight specially loaded LSTs (Landing Ship Tank—'Large Slow Target' in naval parlance) landed at Red Beach just before high tide, and unloaded supplies including the remainder of 'Able' Company Tanks. By the morning of 16 September the two regiments ashore had established contact with each other, forming a solid line around Inchon, while ROK Marines mopped up the port with zealous efficiency.

Further inland a column of six T-34/85s of the NKPA 42nd Mechanised (Tank) Regt. heading towards Inchon was intercepted by Marine Corsairs at the village of Kansong-Ni. Three tanks were disabled by rockets and napalm in the first pass, and a second strike appeared just as successful. The Marine pilots assumed all six tanks were

destroyed, but when 2/5 Marines reached the village in the afternoon this proved to be incorrect. As the infantry approached the final bend into Kangsong-Ni two Pershings were despatched to the top of a hill to cover the advance. From their vantage point the tank crews saw three intact T-34s with hatches closed and guns levelled at the road bend. The Pershings opened fire independently. Desperately the North Koreans tried to elevate and traverse their manually operated guns, but before they could return fire each T-34 was hit by AP rounds and exploded. The Marine attack swept past the blazing wrecks and continued, meeting only light resistance. By evening the two Marine regiments had advanced six miles inland.

During the night of 16–17 September 5th Marines formed a strong defensive position commanding the Seoul highway. Several hundred yards to the rear lay five Pershings, augmented by 3.5 in. bazookas and 75 mm recoilless-rifles. At 0545 six T-34s accompanied by infantry (some of whom rode on the tanks eating their breakfast) were observed advancing along the road, obviously unaware of the situation ahead. The Marines opened fire with every weapon at their disposal while the T-34s were engaged by the Pershings. Within minutes all six enemy tanks were destroyed and 200 of the 250 accompanying

infantry killed—all at a cost of only one wounded Marine.

On the fourth day of the landings 5th Marines captured the vital airfield of Kimpo while 1st Marines continued the advance along the Inchon-Seoul highway, where they met stiff opposition near the village of Mahang-Ri. The lead tank, commanded by 2nd Lt. Bryan Cummings, was hit by anti-tank fire and the engine went dead. The accompanying infantry were driven back by concentrated small-arms and mortar fire. Observing a lone Marine still crouching on his tank Cummings opened the hatch and dragged him into the turret just before enemy infantry surrounded the Pershing. While North Koreans battered on the hull and tried to prise open the hatches, the M26 returned fire with all its weapons, filling the tank with fumes. In the confines of the turret the rescued rifleman went berserk, until his screaming was abruptly halted by a knockout punch from one of the half-

With rifles at the ready, men of No. 1 Ptn. 'A' Co., 1st Bn. Argyll and Sutherland Highlanders ride the rear decks of a Sherman of 'B' Co., 89th Tank Bn. advancing warily through the smoking ruins of Sariwon; 17 October 1950. Not noted for its objective reporting, the Soviet newspaper *Pravda* stated that, '... General MacArthur landed the most arrant criminals at Inchon, gathered from the ends of the earth. ... He sends British and New Zealander adventure-seekers ahead of his own executioners, letting them drag Yankee chestnuts from the fire ...' *(Soldier)*

smothered crew. Desperate for air, Cummings opened the port hatch—whereupon a grenade was thrown in and exploded, wounding three of the trapped men. At that moment a second Pershing arrived and raked Cummings' tank with machine gun fire, killing the swarming North Koreans. Finally the enemy were forced back, leaving 250 dead and wounded and 70 prisoners.

By now other elements of X Corps had landed, including 7th Infantry Div. with 73rd Tank Battalion. This formation took up positions on the Marines' right flank to protect them from enemy units moving up from the south. With Kimpo secured, the UN forces pushed towards Seoul. On the morning of 20 September 5th Marines crossed the Han River in LVTs while 1st Marines fought a fierce battle in the industrial suburb of Yong-dungpo. The North Koreans had resolved to fight for the capital street by street. On the 25th the Marines broke into Seoul in the teeth of extremely heavy resistance. Their attack crept forward house by house. This was the beginning of the so-called 'Battle of the Barricades', for across every street and junction were barriers of earth-filled rice bags rising to eight feet high by five feet

thick. Each was defended by a fanatical detachment of North Koreans, sweeping the streets with anti-tank rounds and machine gun fire. On the rooftops of the houses lining the streets snipers were posted. Marine riflemen had to defend themselves on all sides as their advance settled into a grindingly slow routine. After a preliminary pounding from Marine and Navy aircraft, infantry and mortarmen would set up a base of fire covering the engineers as they removed anti-tank mines. The Pershings then rolled forward engaging the anti-tank guns and automatic weapons, and finally crashing through the barricade. The accompanying infantry gave protection from anti-tank teams, winkled out snipers and cleared the area. A single barricade might hold up a battalion advance for as much as an hour.

Seoul fell on 27 September. Two days later the South Korean government was re-installed in its capital. 1st Marine Div. had not lost a single tank to enemy tank action during the Inchon campaign, although several were lost to mines and infantry action. Approximately 50 T-34s—'Caviar Cans' as they came to be called—were destroyed during the same period, many of them to the 90mm tank fire of the Pershings. With the capture of Seoul, UN forces commanded the railways and major roads supplying Communist troops around the Pusan perimeter. Caught between X Corps and Eighth Army, the NKPA was trapped.

Break-Out from Pusan

On 16 September, in conjunction with the Inchon landings, Eighth Army launched an attack all along the Pusan perimeter in order to prevent enemy units from moving to the Inchon-Seoul sector. This attack also served to break the cordon encircling Eighth Army to enable it to drive northwards to link up with X Corps in the Seoul area. Initially the offensive made only limited progress as the North Koreans, unaware of the threat to their rear, resisted stubbornly. Nevertheless by 20 September UN forces had penetrated the Communist defences, and two days later all units were advancing rapidly northwards.

In most instances the pursuit was undertaken by motorised infantry columns led by tanks. Each force advanced along a single axis, using its speed and mobility to outpace and envelop the plodding enemy. Units such as Task Force Matthews and Task Force Dolvin made spectacular gains despite the mountainous terrain and narrow roads, travelling as much as 200 miles in three days. One of these formations was Task Force Lynch, the lead unit of 1st Cavalry Div. in its attack across the Naktong River. Organised as part of the larger Task Force 777 (named from the first digit of its three principal elements—7th Cavalry Regt., 70th Tank Bn. and 77th Field Artillery Bn.), Task Force Lynch started north on 22 September. With its seven Shermans in the van, the column moved forward while flights of aircraft coursed up and down the road ahead engaging the fleeing enemy. Brushing aside pockets of resistance, the advance made rapid progress and by nightfall had reached the Sonsan ferry. As the task force was preparing to dig in for the night it was diverted to the crossing at Naktong-Ni. Passing through villages set on fire by the retreating North Koreans, the lead tanks reached a bluff overlooking the crossing at 2230, and engaged the enemy rearguard. One

round struck a North Korean ammunition lorry which exploded and burst into flames. The blaze illuminated the surrounding area, revealing numerous abandoned enemy tanks and lorries, some of them still in their original US markings, while below hundreds of retreating North Koreans were attempting to cross the river by a sunken bridge. The ensuing slaughter was considerable as tanks and mortars fired into the closely-packed bodies of men.

The advance continued on the morning of the 26th as Task Force Lynch drove mile after mile without opposition. By late afternoon the six leading tanks had run out of petrol and the advance faltered, although three of them were refuelled by collecting every petrol can in the column. Shortly afterwards, in failing light, three North Korean lorries blundered into the point vehicle and their drivers fled. Providentially the

An M26A1 of Co. 'B', 1st Marine Tank Bn. fords a stream near Hamhung, 10 November 1950—two weeks later this was the scene of the epic withdrawal by the Marines from the Chosin Reservoir battles. The M26A1 can be distinguished from the M26 by the bore evacuator (fume extractor) on its 90mm gun. Stream and river beds were often the only practicable routes for tanks where roads were either non-existent or reserved for wheeled vehicles and infantry, tanks being particularly harmful to the unpaved Korean roads.   (USMC A5240)

Struggling through a blizzard, Shermans of 'A' Co., 89th Tank Bn. retreat along a frozen, snowbound road in the face of the Chinese advance of December 1950. In the vernacular of the time a retrograde manoeuvre such as this was known as 'bugging-out', yet the withdrawal was executed in an orderly if somewhat precipitate manner. While losses of materiel were high, which grieved some of America's allies, casualties were light when compared to similar retreats of the Second World War. *(Soldier)*

lorries were loaded with sufficient petrol to refuel the other three tanks, and the advance resumed along the main Seoul highway at high speed. The leading Shermans began to out-distance the rest of the column and were soon beyond radio contact. With their lights blazing they rumbled through Osan. Some four miles north of the town the crews observed the treads of Pershing tracks on the road, suggesting that American armour was nearby. Suddenly they came under heavy fire. An anti-tank round sheared off the .50cal. machine gun of the third tank and decapitated one of the crew. The Shermans pressed on towards X Corps lines, coming under American small-arms and recoilless-rifle fire. Fortunately the M26s of 73rd Tank Bn. held their fire: the speed, engine noise and headlights of the approaching tanks made the crews doubt whether the interlopers could be the enemy. The unit commander had allowed one tank to pass, with the intention of firing on the second, when a White Phosphorus grenade lit up the white star on the Sherman's side and tragedy

was averted. Eighth Army had made contact with X Corps, at 2226 on 26 September. Task Force Lynch had covered 120 miles in 21 hours, destroying 13 enemy tanks at a cost of two Shermans and two dead.

During the first three months of the war tanks were a crucial factor in the North Korean success and equally so in the UN counter-attack. All combat arms made claims regarding destroyed enemy equipment, especially tanks and AFVs. Those by the Air Force were extravagantly high. A survey conducted in October 1950 below the 38th Parallel reveals a truer picture: 239 destroyed or abandoned T-34s and 74 SU-76 self-propelled guns were discovered, together with 60 knocked-out US tanks.

According to the survey air action destroyed 102 (43 per cent) of enemy tanks, napalm accounting for 60 (25 per cent) of the total. UN tank fire accounted for 39 tanks (16 per cent) and rocket launchers 13 (5 per cent). The latter figure is misleading as air action was undoubtedly credited with many tanks that had originally fallen victim to infantry bazookas. Very few enemy tanks were destroyed by anti-tank mines. Intelligence sources estimated that 242 T-34s were committed to battle in South Korea—by the end of September almost every one of them had been destroyed. In the same period the US suffered 136 tank losses, of which almost 70 per cent were caused by mines, as compared to 20 per cent of tank losses during the Second World War in all theatres of operations. The majority of these casualties were repaired and returned to battle.

North to the Yalu, South to the Imjin

After the collapse of the NKPA in South Korea, the General Assembly of the United Nations resolved on the pursuit and destruction of the enemy within his own territory. By 9 October UN forces had crossed the 38th Parallel with Eighth Army on the left flank astride the main highway between Seoul and Pyongyang, the North Korean capital.

Led by 1st Cavalry Div. with 27th British

After the retreat from Chosin 1st Marine Div. was deployed to the Pohang area of east Korea, where it conducted clearing operations against guerillas and NK soldiers cut off by the UN advance. M26s of Co. 'C' 1st Marine Tank Bn., and an M4A3 105mm Howitzer HVSS tank-dozer without its blade, fire their .50cal. M2HB Brownings against enemy positions in the hills during January 1951. Disease-ridden and starving, hundreds of North Koreans were killed or captured during these 'rice-paddy patrols'. (USMC A6076)

Commonwealth Bde. under operational command, Eighth Army advanced steadily into North Korea, hampered by long and interdicted supply lines from Pusan. By mid-October enemy resistance had waned, and the UN rate of advance averaged ten miles a day over extremely rugged, mountainous terrain ideally suited to defence. The battle for Pyongyang lay ahead—indications were that it would be far more severe than anything encountered so far. Exhorting his troops to defend the city to the last man, Communist premier Kim Il Sung fled to a temporary capital at Sinuiju on the Yalu River.

Every day enemy resistance on the road towards the North Korean capital increased. It was expected that the North Koreans would make a determined stand on the heights of Sariwon protecting the final approaches to Pyongyang. Mounted on the rear decks of Shermans of 89th Tank Bn., 1st Bn. The Argyll and Sutherland Highlanders led the attack on Sariwon. Four miles short of the town enemy rifle fire raked the column from a hillside orchard. The tanks immediately returned fire into the trees and without warning a mass of North Koreans broke and ran, abandoning numerous machine guns and a battery of anti-tank guns. The tanks then entered Sariwon and while 3rd Bn. Royal Australian Regiment (3 RAR) passed through the town to form blocking positions to the north, the Argylls began mopping-up operations.

Throughout the night of 17 October fighting continued amidst considerable confusion: the British were uncertain whether the North Koreans were ROKs attached to 24th Infantry Div. arriving from the south, while the North Koreans thought the Scots in their knitted cap-comforters were Russians! There were several occasions when mutual congratulations and cigarettes were exchanged. In one instance a group of North Koreans greeted a platoon of Argylls with cries of 'Comrade' and, slapping the Highlanders on the back, offered cigarettes and the red stars from their caps as souvenirs. The ensuing fire-fight took place at very close quarters. . . . During that chaotic night in Sariwon about 150 North Koreans were killed and the British lost only one man.

The day before, Task Force Indianhead of 2nd Infantry Div., including six Shermans of 'C' Co., 72nd Tank Bn. entered Pyongyang. It met no

February 1951: a typical Korean scene during the spring thaw as a Marine M4A3 105mm Howitzer HVSS tank-dozer with MIAI dozer-blade gives a helping push to a jeep mired in a mudhole. Many tanks carried prodigious amounts of external stowage for maximum self-sufficiency in case established supply lines were cut by infiltrators or saboteurs. (USMC A6687)

resistance as it rolled through the deserted streets to the radio stations and government buildings, where much valuable intelligence material was discovered. Three days later 1st Cavalry and 1st ROK Divs. reached the city simultaneously. In support of 1st ROK Div. were two companies of 6th Tank Bn. whose M46 Pattons had fought a decisive action near Kojo-Dong some six miles from Pyongyang. In a bitter struggle the tanks of 'C' Co. had destroyed several SU-76s and overrun numerous North Korean entrenchments impeding the ROK advance, crushing enemy infantry and weapons under their tracks.

By the last week of October the NKPA was in parlous straits, with UN forces advancing almost at will. Despite intelligence reports that Chinese 'volunteers' had been identified among North Korean units, optimism ran high. The familiar cry 'Home by Christmas' spread among UN troops. At Ch'ongju on the 29th Shermans of 98th Tank Bn. destroyed four T-34s and an SU-76 in a well-orchestrated envelopment with troops of 3 RAR. Two days later, beyond the

town, seven T-34s and 500 infantry attempted to ambush the column. The nearest enemy tank opened fire at 300 yards. Others joined in. Their orange-tracered shells struck several Shermans but all of them bounced off. The American tanks returned fire, and by dawn had accounted for five T-34s and an SU-76. A similar action took place on the afternoon of 1 November when seven T-34s attacked 1st Bn., 21st Infantry Regt. at Chonggo-Dong. Supporting tanks of 'A' Co., 6th Tank Bn. moved forward to engage the enemy armour and, in a blazing tank battle that lasted half an hour, they destroyed it. This was the northernmost action fought by a tank unit of Eighth Army in the Korean War.

With temperatures dropping below freezing, UN forces advanced slowly for the first three weeks of November against moderate resistance. North Korean units, leavened by increasing numbers of Chinese, fought many rearguard actions, but as the weather worsened operations were conducted on a modest scale. Several UN units reached the Yalu River, across which they could see the barren landscape of Manchuria.

On 24 November UN forces launched an offensive that was intended to conclude the war. Things went well for 24 hours, but that night the Chinese Communist Forces (CCF) struck in strength across the entire front, exploiting the ga between Eighth Army and X Corps. By 28 November 30 Chinese divisions had enveloped the forward UN units. Using human-wave tactics, they forced the defenders to withdraw to avoid complete encirclement and destruction. Eighth Army broke contact and fell back. The abominable weather and primitive roads clogged with refugees pouring southwards seriously hampered the retreat. The tanks, confined to the narrow, icy tracks, faced appalling difficulties. The precipitous hills that a few weeks previously had been a difficult impediment were now an insurmountable obstacle. Tank-tracks skated helplessly on the frozen ground, and a vehicle that slipped off the road could hold up those behind for hours on end. Desperate measures were improvised to enable tanks to negotiate the steep, glacial hills. Gallons of anti-freeze were poured down the slopes, or else they were flooded with petrol and set alight to melt the surface sufficiently for tank tracks to grip. With temperatures dropping to below −20°F an added misery was the wind-chill factor, which reduced the temperature by one degree for every mile per hour of wind. Crew members exposed in turrets or driving compartments were tormented by frozen dust particles thrown up by the tracks and whipped into their faces by the howling wind.

By the end of 1950, Eighth Army had withdrawn some 150 miles and had taken up positions across the peninsula south of the 38th Parallel, but the situation remained critical. The CCF, whose pursuit was slow due to their reliance on human and animal transport, resumed the attack on New Year's Day. Eighth Army was forced back once more. On 4 January Seoul fell, but by the end of the month the attack was contained. The

'B.J.', an M4A3 HVSS POA-CWS-H5 Flamethrower of 1st Marine Tank Bn., advances on the central Korean front in the Wonju-Hoensong area, 23 February 1951. With the fuel tanks for the flame projector carried inside the vehicle space was severely restricted, and ammunition for the 105mm howitzer was limited to 20 rounds. Mounted in the mantlet beside the 105mm, the flamethrower had an effective range of 100 yards with a capacity of approximately 80 one-second bursts. Marine flamethrowers were organised in Flame Sections within Headquarters and Service Companies of Marine Tank Battalions. (USMC A6876)

Infantrymen scramble for cover as mortar fire falls near an M4A3(76)W HVSS of 32nd Regimental Combat Team, 7th Infantry Div. which has just run over an anti-tank mine on the outskirts of Hadaewa; 28 February 1951. Almost 70 per cent of UN tank casualties were caused by mines. Often of crude construction, the wooden box-mines were virtually impossible to detect with electromagnetic mine detectors, and no effective counter-measures were found against them. Detection was only guaranteed by laborious probing with bayonets. The .30cal.M1919 Browning machine guns were frequently mounted forward of the commander's cupola to allow him to fire a weapon from within the turret, rather than exposed on the engine decks as was necessary with the .50cal. on its 'sky-mount'. (US Army SC359465)

Chinese had suffered enormous casualties; their troops had been decimated by smallpox and frostbite and their supply lines were constantly attacked by UN airpower.

During the next two months Eighth Army mounted a series of attacks intended to inflict the maximum casulaties on the extended enemy. 'Operation Killer' of February was followed by 'Operation Ripper' in March as UN forces advanced northwards along the entire front, pushing the Communists back across the Han River and exacting a great toll of men and equipment. During these attacks many American tanks were decorated with ferocious painted tigers or dragons to mark the Chinese New Year and to instil fear in the supposedly superstitious enemy.

Whether these colour-schemes had any effect on enemy morale is doubtful; but the relentless advance of tank-infantry task forces in conjunction with artillery and aircraft inflicted heavy losses on the Communists with the minimum of casualties. The enemy, however, was far from beaten, and his much-heralded spring offensive was expected at any time.

Battle of the Imjin River

By the light of a full moon in the early hours of 22 April three Chinese armies attacked the UN lines. The main effort was launched against I and IX Corps in the western sector, with the intention of capturing Seoul and enveloping the greater part of I Corps. Directly in the path of this offensive lay 29th British Independent Brigade.

The 29th Brigade, with the Belgian Battalion under operational command, was holding the line of the Imjin River from Choksong on the left to the junction of the Imjin and Hantan rivers on the right—a frontage of some 12,000 yards. The brigade front was neither wired nor mined as it was looked upon as only a phase-line in the general advance. From right to left the infantry battalions were disposed as follows: 1st Bn. Royal Northumberland Fusiliers, 1st Bn. The Royal Ulster Rifles and 1st Bn. The Gloucestershire Regiment. The Fusiliers and Ulsters were on the right and left respectively of the Main Supply Route (MSR), with the Belgians on the north bank of the Imjin. The Gloucesters were on the left of the brigade front, separated from the other battalions by a high ridge of hills dominated by the rugged mass of Kamak-San, some 2,000 feet high. In the event of attack the Belgians were to fall back south of the river to a position between the Fusiliers and Gloucesters. In support of the Brigade were the Centurions of 'C' Sqn., 8th King's Royal Irish Hussars (8 KRIH) and the 25-pdrs. of 45th Field Regiment, RA.

Fording the waist-deep Imjin, the Chinese attacked in great force, and the Belgians north of the river were soon cut off. During the first hours of the battle the tanks lay immobile in their leaguer at Mistletoe Orchard, lapped by the furious gunfire to the front and the constant barrage of the 25-pdrs. to their left. Throughout the night the forward battalions were heavily engaged. When day came the tanks joined in the battle, escorting counter-attacks by the hard-pressed Fusiliers and providing smokescreens and fire support as required. The main attack, however, was being directed against the Belgians and Gloucesters, who were beyond the reach of the tanks.

That night the Belgians fought their way back across the river, but by morning the Gloucesters found themselves completely surrounded. Some of the 'C' Sqn. Centurions, led by Major Henry Huth, supported by a detachment of Filipinos and three M24 Chaffees now made a desperate attempt to relieve them. Impossible going and

'Colt-45', an M4A3(76)W HVSS of 'C' Co., 89th Tank Bn. with a flamethrower in place of the bow machine gun, engages a cave harbouring Chinese infantry in the Han River area, 9 March 1951. The spare bogiewheel on the turret side and sprocket ring brackets on the hull sponson indicate that this was one of the original Shermans of the battalion, salvaged after the Second World War and refurbished in Japan.
(US Army SC361283)

The crew of 'Suits Me', an M4A3(76)W HVSS of 17th Tank Co., 17th Regimental Combat Team, 7th Infantry Div., observe an airstrike against Chinese positions north of Singpung-Ni, 7 April 1951. The nearer crewman wears a .45cal.M1911A1 automatic pistol in a black leather shoulder holster, and on his crash helmet the insignia of Eighth Army, a white Maltese cross on a red shield.   (US Army SC363979)

enemy bazooka fire brought their advance to a halt, and the column was forced to reverse along the narrow track for over a mile before being able to turn.

The remainder of 'C' Sqn., under Capt. Peter Ormrod, had been in action all day, exposing their tanks in counter-attacks without infantry support; but Chinese pressure built up relentlessly. By nightfall the Fusiliers and Ulsters were in imminent danger of being cut off, and plans were made to break through to them in the morning. 'Ormrodforce'—consisting of 1, 3 and 4 Troops and the Carrier Troop plus the two tanks of RHQ—was to open the road up the valley and give close support to the Fusiliers and Ulsters, while 2 Troop was to support the Belgian position. The squadron commander's tank, a Gunner OP Cromwell and two other Centurions were to act as reserve as well as reconnoitring alternative escape routes eastwards.

Throughout the night the Gloucesters were subjected to repeated attacks within their shrinking perimeter. In the early hours the Chinese also attacked the Ulsters on the hills to the right of the MSR and the Belgians to the left, with the object of enveloping the brigade and cutting the road to Uijongbu. At 0500 the Centurions of Ormrod-force prepared to move out of leaguer, but their departure was delayed half an hour by heavy ground mist. 3 Troop (Lt. M. Radford) and 4 Troop (Lt. J. Hurst) drove to the pass without difficulty. 4 Troop took up position to cover any

threat from the northern re-entrant to the west of the road. 1 Troop (Lt. P. Boyall), and the Carrier Troop carrying Sappers of 55 Field Sqn. RE acting as infantry, covered the southern re-entrant to the west of the road. Beyond the pass 3 Troop came under heavy mortar fire which forced the commanders to close down. Persistent ground mist obscured their vision, and '3 Baker' and '3 Charlie' ran off the road into the paddy fields. One tank managed to stop but the other ploughed on, shedding both its tracks. '3 Baker' was recovered by 1200, but '3 Charlie' had to be destroyed by Capt. Gavin Murray at 1230 as being impossible to rescue.

Working in steep, rocky terrain without infantry support, the tanks were open to attack at close range. There were approximately 200 enemy in the killing ground. One Chinaman threw a sticky bomb at Lt. Radford's Centurion 'Colombo', blowing a hole in the sideplate, but the suspension was undamaged and Radford moved on, oblivious to this nuisance. The Chinese swarmed through the rocks and bushes, rushing the tanks and trying to force hatches open to drop grenades inside, but the closed-down Centurions swept each others hulls and turrets with co-axial Besa fire. Capt. Ormrod and Sgt. Reeckie in '3 Able' switched to the offensive and forced the Chinese to run. A group of them took shelter in an abandoned house but were destroyed by two rounds of HE. The fight in the trap continued with the six Centurions, aided by Cornet John Venner in a Dingo, sweeping the entire area with fire and forcing the Chinese to withdraw out of reach.

4 Troop, which had been sent further up the road, ran into trouble of its own and a brisk action took place, but once again the Centurions beat off their ambushers. The remnants of the opposition broke and ran straight towards Capt. Ormrod's tank as it emerged from the area of the first trap. One Chinese with a sticky bomb was crushed under his tracks. 1 and 4 Troops then remained covering the northern and southern re-entrants for the next four and a half hours, while the enemy tried continually to stalk and ambush them.

The Corps Commander arrived at Brigade HQ at 1000, and informed Brig. Brodie that an attempt by 65th RCT to relieve the Gloucesters had failed. This left Brigade HQ open to attack, as the Belgian battalion protecting the position was now heavily outnumbered. At 1030 the brigade was ordered to withdraw as the enemy pressure was too great. Ammunition and water were running low and radio batteries exhausted.

The Fusiliers started to withdraw under the covering fire of the tanks and escaped without further casualties. The first company of Ulsters also moved out without difficulty. The enemy threat from the north-west was very real and the road was under heavy and accurate mortar fire. The remainder of the Ulsters struck out south-east over the hills and so avoided the area of the pass. 1 Troop was now at the pass with the troop leader's tank perched like a chamois atop a small hill, lashing out at the enemy who were building up in the southern re-entrant to the west of the road. This was the critical hour. A wave of Chinese swept down from the hills all along the west of the valley, forcing the tank commanders to close down. Lt. Radford, to the north, reported that the enemy were all over the valley floor. There was a very real danger that all the tanks would be trapped within this teeming cauldron. The Centurions ran the gauntlet of the treacherous ground. Sgt. Reekie's '3 Able' was knocked out by a sticky bomb and Sgt. Holberton's '4 Baker' was disabled when, in an attempt to evade Chinese anti-tank teams, it careered over a steep dyke, spiking its gun in the ground.

Meanwhile 1 Troop was struggling to keep the pass open, ably supported by about 30 Sappers and the Ulster Reserve Company. As the infantry withdrew through the pass 1 Troop pulled out, bringing some of the Ulsters with them as well as the Sapper escort, running the gauntlet of Chinese troops either side of the road for about a mile. Many of the infantry on the backs of the tanks were wounded. At this point the hard-pressed Belgians were ordered to withdraw under the covering fire of 2 Troop, which had given them excellent support all morning. As they pulled out, with the Centurions firing to the rear at the advancing enemy, '2 Able' (Sgt. Ripley) stuck in reverse gear, crawling backwards at less than walking pace. When told of this Major Huth gave permission for it to be destroyed, but the Belgian colonel refused. The rate of withdrawal slowed to

Similar in configuration to the M7 Priest, the M37 Howitzer Motor Carriage was based on the chassis of the M24 Chaffee and entered service in the closing days of the Second World War. Here, M37s of 58th Field Artillery Bn. fire their 105mm howitzers across the Imjin River in support of 3rd Infantry Div. on 12 April 1951. With an air-recognition panel draped across the glacis plate, the nearer vehicle sports a large cartoon on the machine gun pulpit depicting a flaming devil with the name 'Hell Fire' above. (US Army SC363745)

keep pace with the lame tank, which eventually reached the night-leaguer area, where the Centurions came under Major Huth's direct control.

At the same time, 'Ormrodforce' had fought its way along the last lap of the valley through masses of Chinese, as 2,000 or more swarmed down from the west in an attempt to cut them off. The Centurions surged on, crushing enemy soldiers under their tracks. Sgt. Cadman in '26 Able', an RHQ tank, hearing a Chinaman battering at his cupola hatch, directed his Centurion through the wall of a building to brush him off and then ran over a machine gun emplacement beside the road. Suddenly three platoons of enemy infantry rose up out of a river bed in parade ground order, only to be blown to oblivion with some of the last rounds. Some tanks took to the treacherous paddy fields. Few of the infantry riding on the rear decks survived this death-ride. The tanks finally debouched from the valley and limped into the squadron leaguer area: 'the Centurions piled high with dead and wounded . . . blood ran down their sides turning the dust into crimson mud'.

Major Huth ordered 'Ormrodforce' to pass straight through to seek help for the wounded while he organised the withdrawal of the remainder of 'C' Squadron. In an effort to speed the evacuation of 2 Troop's lame 'Able', Lt. Ted Paul took it under tow. While the tow-line was being attached Chinese machine gun fire from the hills some 50 yards away struck an 88 White Phosphorus grenade in the smoke discharger cups of the troop leader's tank, 'Chaucer'. As the turret was traversed at the time, burning phosphorus flowed over the engine louvres, setting the engine on fire. With the Chinese only 30 yards away the crews baled out under covering fire from Major Huth. He then fired an AP round through each tank, and quickly traversed his turret left to engage the fast-approaching enemy. For three deliberate minutes the turret of 'Cameronian' swung this way and that, firing long bursts of Besa into the Chinese. Only when it became absolutely necessary did Major Huth order his driver to

One of the hazards in the mountainous terrain of Korea was the soft shoulders of roads collapsing under the weight of tanks, leading on some occasions to spectacular plunges down precipitous hillsides. This Sherman of 17th Tank Co., 17th Regimental Combat Team, 7th Infantry Div. is safely lodged against a tree, and recovery is being made by a late-production M32B1 TRV (Tank Recovery Vehicle) on 15 April 1951.   (US Army SC363842)

retire. A hundred yards further back he was joined by Lt. John Lidsey in the other RHQ tank, and together they continued the delaying action until there was an acceptable distance between the retreating infantry and the enemy. The two tanks rapidly pulled back half a mile down the road, to a new crisis.

Exhausted and wounded Ulsters were struggling towards the road from the hills to the east. Ordering those tanks which had halted in the vicinity to load to capacity with the infantrymen and withdraw, Major Huth and Lt. Lidsey moved forward again in an attempt to force the enemy back. For almost an hour the two Centurions fought a brilliant and courageous rearguard action. Each time the Chinese infantry were about to outflank the point tank it withdrew some 200 yards under the covering fire of the other. The Chinese followed the tanks in swarms at distances of frequently less than 50 yards, quite oblivious to their casualties. Major Huth measured his fire-

power against the speed of the approaching enemy so accurately that he imposed the minimum rate of advance upon them, allowing the infantry precious minutes to gain safety. Two other tanks eventually arrived to strengthen the rearguard, but not until the last infantryman was seen to reach the safety of the MSR, where more powerful firepower was available to them, did Major Huth give the order to withdraw. The last shot by Major Huth ended the battle of the Imjin River.

'Only the Gloucesters had not withdrawn. At dawn on the 25th the Gloucesters with their wounded and dead about them were still on Hill 235. The guns of 45th Field Regiment had given them protection all night, and before sunrise Col. Carne told the drum-major to blow a long reveille. Roland's horn among the mountains, gathering echoes from centuries of battle, sounded again, and the haggard soldiers on their blackened hillside rose and cheered. Then the assault came in again . . .'[1] That night the Gloucesters

[1] *Our Men in Korea.* Eric Linklater. HMSO.

received permission to break out, but, totally encircled by thousands of Chinese, few were able to do so and the remainder were captured. The brigade had lost a quarter of its strength, but had it not been for the Centurions of the 8th Hussars it is unlikely that the Belgians, Fusiliers or Ulsters could have been saved.

For their part in the action Capts. Ormrod and Murray and Cornet Venner were awarded the MC, Major Huth MC the DSO, and Lt. Radford was mentioned in despatches.

The 64th Tank Bn.* of 3rd Infantry Div. arrived in Korea in November 1950; the asterisk denotes a Negro unit. Desegregation of units began in earnest in 1951. An M46 tows a crippled companion through Uijongbu as UN forces withdraw during the Chinese spring offensive, 27 April 1951. Characteristic of this unit, tank numbers on the turrets are striped diagonally white and blue, the colours of the shoulder patch of 3rd Infantry Division. (US Army SC365755)

21

Hill-Fighting and Bunker-Busting

The failure of the 1951 Chinese spring offensive demonstrated that the Communists did not have the capacity to defeat Eighth Army on the field of battle. In June the Soviet Union indicated it was willing to seek a settlement in Korea through arbitration. Negotiations began on 10 July in the city of Kaesong and subsequently at Panmunjon; but a further two years were to elapse before an armistice was agreed.

Throughout this time neither side launched major offensive ground operations, but the fighting continued in a monotonous routine of patrol clashes, raids and bitter small-unit struggles for key positions. By the end of 1951 a lull had settled over the battlefield, with the opposing sides occupying defence lines based on major terrain features and stretching the breadth of the Korean peninsula. Not until the summer of 1953 was the fighting resumed on an intensive scale, and then only briefly as the Communists attempted to capture certain important positions before the armistice. Nonetheless, actions such as Bloody Ridge, Old Baldy, the Hook and Porkchop Hill were some of the fiercest battles of the war.

For the tanks this new form of warfare denied them their advantage of mobility, and they were employed for the most part as static, front-line artillery. Their most frequent task was the destruction of enemy bunkers. Tanks were positioned in prepared firing sites on the Main Line of Resistance (MLR) which were invariably on high ground, with wide fields of fire to exploit fully the capabilities of the tanks' main armament.

In the appalling terrain of Korea's mountain regions the scaling of hills to these firing positions posed intractable problems. On many occasions tanks attempting to negotiate a steep hillside shed their tracks, often sliding for hundreds of feet down the hill in a shower of rocks and dirt. The only sure way to climb hills was to drive straight up without turning in motion. To help their M4A3E8s claw their way up mountain trails, crews often welded centre-guides from M46 Patton tracks upside down on their tracklinks. Spaced about five blocks apart, the centre-guides acted as four-inch grousers for greater traction. These improvisations were decidedly unpopular with engineers as they damaged roads and trails, rendering them unserviceable to other vehicles.

Once perched hull-down on the skyline tanks were not moved except for maintenance or in cases where the terrain permitted alternative firing sites. In western Korea it proved expedient to position tanks in defiladed assembly areas, where they were on call and ready to move into their firing sites at short notice. Since tanks under enemy observation invariably drew retaliatory fire, they usually remained in firing positions on the MLR only long enough to complete their fire mission. Earthworks, sandbags and dirt-filled ammunition containers protected suspensions and tracks against enemy artillery. In hotly contested positions overhead cover of timber beams was constructed. Many crews laid a carpet of sandbags over the engine decks as protection from mortar bombs. Beside each tank were ammunition bunkers containing up to 200 rounds sufficient for sustained operations when supply routes were temporarily impassable due to enemy action or inclement weather. Ammunition supply to the hilltop positions was a constant problem and it was often necessary to resort to pack animals and South Korean porters. The M39 Armoured Utility Vehicle was frequently employed on this duty, as was the M29C Weasel

With its high floatation and low gear ratios the Weasel proved a very satisfactory ammunition carrier, transporting 30 to 40 rounds of 76mm in fibre cases up the steepest tracks.

For tactical purposes, the tanks of the regimental tank companies and divisional tank battalions were placed under operational control of the infantry regiments. They were positioned along the entire sector rather than clustered in platoon-sized units. Wherever possible their positions were mutually supporting and selected to permit concentration of a maximum number of tanks on a designated target area. As the infantry commander was in radio contact with the armour commander and all tanks in the sector operated on the same frequency, a fire plan could be adjusted rapidly against a given target. In their capacity as direct fire weapons tanks supplemented the artillery by firing H and I (Harassing and Interdiction) missions, and undertook pre-registered defensive fire plans on call from the infantry.

Since the enemy was wholly dependent on ground observation to direct his guns and mortars on allied positions, the primary objective of the tanks was the destruction of his forward OPs (Observation Posts). Once these positions were neutralised, the volume and accuracy of enemy artillery fire were seriously reduced. The enemy defence was based on a system of bunkers constructed on the topographical crest of dominant terrain. The forward slopes were usually occupied with foxholes, with a few machine gun nests for close protection of the main battle line. To the rear, however, the enemy constructed bunkers by tunnelling through from the back of hills and enlarging sections of the tunnel into shelters and casemates. This produced emplacements of great natural strength, and, since the work did not disturb the soil and natural growth on a hill, they

Each tank company in Korea had a tank-dozer to undertake the numerous earth-moving and route-improvement tasks that were crucial to mobility in such terrain. An M4A3(76)W HVSS tank-dozer with M2 dozer-blade of 7th Reconnaissance Co., 7th Infantry Div., fills a crater on a road near Chunchon, 24 May 1951. (US Army SC367592)

were well camouflaged. To counter them UN forces undertook a systematic campaign of bunker destruction, known as 'bunker-busting', with all available weapons.

The inexperience of tank crews led inevitably to much wastage of ammunition but, gradually, efficient techniques were developed. The initial problem was the location of the firing embrasure or OP. As the magnification of the tank gunsight was often insufficient for this task, high-power telescopes and binocular periscopes were employed in addition to reconnaissance by fire. Once the exact location had been determined the information was plotted on a sketch, overlay or map. Many crews made cardboard panorama silhouettes of the terrain to their front from C-ration wrappers, pin-pointing enemy positions so that any new diggings were readily apparent after a quick visual check. Since the firing slit or OP was usually camouflaged it was first necessary to

---

US and British Commonwealth Armoured Units in the Korean War
(excluding Reconnaissance Companies and Regimental Tank Companies)

Unit:	Assigned to:
US Army	
6th Medium Tk.Bn. (Redesignated 6th Tk.Bn., 10–11–51)	24th Inf.Div.
56th Amphib. Tk. & Tractor Bn.	X Corps
64th Heavy Tk.Bn.* (Re-organised & redesignated 64th Tk.Bn.*, 6–3–51; same title on desegregation)	3rd Inf.Div. (10–11–51)
70th Heavy Tk.Bn. (Re-orgn. & redes. 70th Tk.Bn., 2–5–50)	1st Cav.Div. (10–11–50)
Co.'A'.71st Heavy Tk.Bn. (Re-org. & redes. 71st Tk.Bn., 5–8–50; inactivated, 16–10–50)	1st Cav.Div.
72nd Heavy Tk.Bn. (Re-org. & redes. 72nd Tk.Bn., 6–6–50)	2nd Inf.Div.
73rd Heavy Tk.Bn. (Redes.73rd Tk.Bn., 14–7–50)	3rd Inf.Div.; 7th Inf.Div., 10–11–51
77th Heavy Tk.Bn. (Re-org. & redes. 77th Tk.Bn., 5–8–50; inactivated, 10–11–51)	7th Inf.Div.
8072nd Medium Tk.Bn. (Re-org. & redes. 89th Medium Tk.Bn., 7–8–50; 89th Tk.Bn., 14–11–51)	25th Inf.Div.
(* = Negro unit)	
140th Tk.Bn. (29–12–51)	40th Div., (California) National Guard
245th Tk.Bn. (3–2–52)	45th Div., (Oklahoma) NG
1st Marine Tk.Bn.	1st Marine Div.,USMC
1st Marine Amphib.Tractor Bn.	1st Marine Div.,USMC
1st Marine Armd. Amphib.Tractor Bn.	1st Marine Div.,USMC
Commonwealth	
8th King's Royal Irish Hussars (Nov.50 —Dec.51)	29th British Independent Bde.; 1st Commonwealth Div.,28–7–51
'C'Sqn.,7th Royal Tk.Regt. (Nov.50—Oct.51)	As above
'C'Sqn.,Lord Strathcona's Horse (Royal Canadians)(2nd Armd.Regt.) (May 51—June 52)	25th Canadian Inf.Bde., 1st Commonwealth Div.
5th Royal Inniskilling Dragoon Gds. (Dec.51—Dec.52)	1st Commonwealth Div.
'B'Sqn.,Lord Strathcona's Horse (June 52—May 53)	As 'C'Sqn. LSH,above
1st Royal Tk.Regt. (Dec.52—Dec.53)	1st Commonwealth Div.
'A' Sqn.,Lord Strathcona's Horse (May 53—ECH)	As 'C' Sqn. LSH, above
5th Royal Tk. Regt. (Dec.53—Dec.54)	1st Commonwealth Div.

미 제침략자들을소멸하라!

1: T-34/85, NKPA 109th Armd.Regt.,
105th Armd.Bde.; Seoul, 27-6-50

2: M24 Chaffee, 24th Recce Co.,
US 24th Inf.Div.; Chonui, 10-7-50

A

1: M26, 1st Pltn.,Co.'B', 1st Marine Tk.Bn. USMC; Seoul, 27-9-50

2: M4A3(76)W HVSS, Co.'C', 72nd Tk.Bn., US 2nd Inf.Div.

B

M4A3(76)W HVSS Shermans, March-April 1951:
1: Co.'C', 89th Tk.Bn.
2: 64th Tk.Bn.
3: Co.'A', 70th Tk.Bn.
4: Tank Co.,65th Regtl.Combat Team

C

1: Cromwell Mk VII OP, 45th Field Regt. RA;
Battle of Happy Valley, 3-1-51

2 and 3: Daimler Dingo Mk II Scout Car and
Universal Carrier No 1 Mk III, 'C'Sqn., 8th King's
Royal Irish Hussars; Battle of the Imjin River,
22-25 April '51.

D

1: M46 Patton, Co.'B', 6th Tk.Bn., US 24th Inf.Div.:
Munsan-ni, March 1951

2: M4A3 Dozer Tank, HQ & Service Co., 3rd Eng.Bn.,
US 24th Inf.Div.; March 1951

E

1: Centurion Mk 3, 1 Tp., 'C' Sqn., 5th Royal Inniskilling Dragoon Guards;
Operation 'Jehu', 17-6-52

2: M4A3(76)W HVSS, 'C'Sqn., Lord Strathcona's Horse; Sami-chon, Nov. 1951

F

1: M40, Bty,'C', 937th Field Arty.Bn.; April 1951

2: M41, Bty.'A', 92nd Armd. Field Arty.Bn.; April 1951

1: M19, Bty. 'B', 3rd Anti-Aircraft Artillery Automatic Weapons Bn., US 3rd Inf. Div.; August '52

3: M15A1, Turkish Bde.; June 1951

2: M16, Bty. 'B', 15th AAAW Bn., US 7th Inf. Div.; March '51

H

remove all natural growth from the area. This was achieved by airstrikes of napalm to burn away the vegetation or, alternatively, artillery and mortar attacks with 'quick fuse' HE or White Phosphorus (WP). Tanks also stripped camouflage with HE and WP shells, but this was only done when other means were not available.

Once the embrasure was exposed several rounds of 'quick fuse' HE were fired through the slit, followed by a few rounds of 'fuse delay' HE and WP to inflict casualties among the enemy gun crew or OP team who might have withdrawn into the interior of their position. This procedure was known as 'posting letters'. This being achieved, the destruction of the bunker proceeded, to prevent re-occupation. A combination of APC and 'fuse delay' HE rounds were fired at the top of the embrasure and a few feet below it. This 'pick and shovel' process led to the collapse of the entire structure. The APC round—'the pick'— travelled at great velocity, smashing the logs supporting the roof and floor, while the HE round —'the shovel'—blew the loosened material downwards and upwards along the path of least resistance into the chamber itself. The Communists constructed numerous dummy bunkers intended to deplete UN ammunition supplies.

Once a bunker had been destroyed it was necessary to ensure that it was not repaired. The enemy invariably undertook repair work at night, so tanks continued to harass known positions throughout the hours of darkness. Many tanks were fitted with searchlights over the main armament. As the smoke and muzzle blast of firing obscured the light beam tanks were usually employed in pairs, one illuminating a target while the other engaged it with HE.

Because of the accuracy of their direct fire and the armour protection afforded to crews in the exposed positions, tanks were the best means available for 'bunker-busting'. Although all tanks were employed for this task the heavier armament of the M46 Patton and the Centurion proved more effective than that of the more numerous M4A3E8 Sherman. It was realised that the 76mm projectile was too light, necessitating a greater expenditure of ammunition and rapid wear of gun barrels. 155mm self-propelled guns and 8in. self-propelled howitzers firing in the direct rôle were also used in

Many of the AFVs employed in Korea were of Second World War vintage, such as this M7B1 105mm Howitzer Motor Carriage of 'C' Battery, 300th Field Artillery Bn. firing in support of 1st Marine Div. during the battle for Hill 785, near Injeon 22 September 1951. A number of these vehicles were modified during the war by raising the howitzer mounting to increase the maximum elevation from +35 to +65 degrees; this conversion, designated M7B2, made easier the placing of indirect fire on the reverse slopes of steep Korean hills. (US Army SC381292)

the 'bunker-busting' campaign, with devastating effect.

Enemy counter-measures against the tanks relied on the massive concentration of artillery and mortars on individual positions. This was largely ineffective as the tanks on the ridge lines were a difficult target to hit with indirect fire. Any rounds that fell short caused no damage, and rounds falling in the valley to the rear of the tanks were impossible to plot as the enemy had no aerial spotters. Only infrequently were tanks hit by any calibre of weapon capable of inflicting significant damage, and few experienced tank crews were inconvenienced. However, their sense of security was not shared by neighbouring infantry as a Sapper on the Hook position testifies: 'Limited armoured support was available but was not always welcomed. Once targets had been spotted, usually by day, on the opposing hills, a Centurion tank would creep up to the crest and fire two or three rounds before retiring behind the hill and closing down against the inevitable enemy re-action. Unfortunately they rarely seemed to think about lesser mortals going about their normal routine, and enemy retribution resulted in frantic dives for cover and interrupted tasks.

Mounted on earth ramps to increase the maximum elevation of the 76mm guns, Shermans of 23rd Tank Co., 23rd Infantry Regt., 2nd Infantry Div. fire as artillery against Chinese positions north of Pia-ri, 18 September 1951 — a frequent rôle for tanks during the Korean War. The Shermans are painted in the summer camouflage scheme of irregular earth-brown stripes over the base colour of olive drab.
(US Army SC 380799)

Tanks were not popular.' Enemy tank-hunter teams also operated under the cover of darkness. Armed with rocket launchers and anti-tank grenades, they attempted to infiltrate tank positions; but these efforts were frustrated by installing extensive barbed wire entanglements, anti-personnel mines and trip flares forward of firing sites. These passive measures, combined with alert guards and tank-mounted searchlights, effectively reduced the threat to nuisance level.

Another important task for tanks was the support of infantry raids or patrols in 'No Man's Land'. These raids were usually conducted to capture prisoners for intelligence purposes or to destroy enemy positions beyond the reach of support weapons. In these circumstances the tanks provided fire support, registering targets during the day and firing on fixed lines at night. A patrol or raiding party gave the codeword by radio and covering fire was rapidly brought to bear. Fire support from main armament and machine guns was often delivered within 25

yards of friendly infantry. A favoured weapon of tank crews was the .50cal. M2HB Browning, not only for its volume and accuracy of fire at distant targets but also for its devastating effect against massed infantry. Some tanks mounted twin .50 cals. on the turret and another in the hull machine gun position. Self-propelled anti-aircraft guns were also employed along the MLR to deliver a high volume of accurate fire at intermediate ranges, adding depth to both offensive and defensive fire plans.

Despite the almost static employment of tanks during this period, some armoured raids were undertaken, usually with limited objectives in mind such as the destruction of enemy positions hidden from direct fire. On 17 June 1952 Operation 'Jehu' was mounted by two troops of 'C' Sqn., 5th Royal Inniskilling Dragoon Guards, with two infantry sections of 1st Bn. Princess Patricia's Canadian Light Infantry and a detachment of Sappers carried in two 'Tugs' (turretless Centurions used as personnel carriers, supply vehicles, and for medical evacuation). The objective was Point 156, which was believed to be a battalion position with numerous mortars on its reverse slope.

Early on 17 June Sappers breached the mine fields and wire and by 0500 1 Troop, 'C' Sqn. had crossed the start line while fire from 'B' Sqn.

26

Lord Strathcona's Horse broke down the 'bund' beyond the stream which ran through the valley facing the objective. 1 Troop's passage through the paddy field and stream churned the area into a quagmire. Three Centurions of 4 Troop coming up behind were soon bogged. The advance was resumed by 1 Troop and the remaining tank of 4 Troop, with '1 Able' commanded by Sgt. James Bertrand leading. After destroying a mountain gun which had opened fire at close range, Sergeant Bertrand recalls: 'I found myself running up a fairly narrow spur with a long enemy communication trench dangerously near the tank track and, to cap it all, the danger of a bunker collapsing under the weight of a 50-ton Centurion was also a possibility.'

Baulked by a rocky spur 100 yards short of the final objective, the Centurions were still able to fire on bunkers normally hidden from friendly eyes. One shot revealed an enormous bunker which immediately received the full attention of all the tanks and the divisional artillery. At 0630 the order was given to withdraw, which meant, in the words of Sgt. Bertrand, 'a perilous return to our own lines. The route out through the minefield had unfortunately been blocked by a tank minus its tracks, thus necessitating a return over the face of Point 159 at a speed of about 3mph and through another of our own minefields. This of course delighted the enemy guns who, for what seemed like hours to the tank crews involved, had good targets to engage.' Within an hour the raiding force had returned safely except for the

The M39 Armoured Utility Vehicle was used extensively throughout the Korean War in rôles such as personnel carrier, medical evacuation and supply. It was also employed as a mobile mounting for various weapons including the M55 quad .50 or as in this case, the 81mm mortar. The vehicle illustrated was converted by the Reconnaissance Ptn., HQ Co., 72nd Tank Bn., 2nd Infantry Division.
(US Army SC397518)

three tanks stuck in the valley below.

The recovery of these bogged tanks was an operation in itself. The first ARV on the scene ran over a mine as enemy artillery pounded the area. A second ARV was sent forward, but its winch rope was cut by shell-fire and the EME officer directing the recovery operation wounded. A medical 'Tug' set out, but it too bogged down, bringing the total to 'five in the mire being shelled'. By dint of hard work under fire, three of the five were recovered by the end of the day. The recovery of the two remaining Centurions took several days longer. While infantry patrols guarded the tanks by night, Sappers cleared the minefields and bulldozed a new track under a continuous smokescreen from divisional artillery. Eventually ARVs were able to extricate the casualties. Despite the undoubted success of

Operation 'Jehu', the subsequent expenditure of considerable divisional resources in the recovery of the bogged tanks outweighed the damage inflicted on the enemy, and such raids were rarely repeated.

The Tank Driver's War

This operation illustrates the problems of mobility that plagued tank crews in Korea. The skill of the driver and tank commander in negotiating the hazardous terrain was paramount to the success of any mission. The following recollections of tank drivers of the 140th Tank Bn. indicate the difficulties they faced in combat:

'Combat tank driving consists mostly of maintenance and good judgement. Driving the M46 after training in an M4 is like stepping from a Model-T Ford into a new Cadillac. The controls are very sensitive and react to your slightest pressure; but the M46 has special driving problems, different from an M4. You just can't jerk the driving controls the way you can on an M4 or you will probably break the final drives. And

'Cottage II', a Centurion Mk. 3 of 3 Tp., 'C' Sqn., 8th King's Royal Irish Hussars, claws its way to the summit of a hill, from where it can dominate the surrounding terrain. The outstanding agility of Centurion and the accuracy of its 20 pdr. main armament won widespread renown in Korea. (See Vanguard No. 22 *The Centurion Tank in Battle*)**.** *(Soldier)*

when you are shifting from high to low, you have to be careful not to put it in reverse and tear up the transmission. It is pretty slow on climbing hills but I must admit it has climbed any I have tried. On flat ground the M46 is a fast tank and easy to manoeuvre.

'The terrain in Korea is rocky, muddy and hilly. The roads here are in bad shape. In many places creeks are used for roads. The creek beds are rocky and you have to be careful not to throw a track—especially on turns. We have to ford streams and small rivers constantly, and that's hard on lubricants. After each mission our tanks are greased thoroughly. Maintenance is quite a problem over here. Parts were hard to get when we arrived, and we really had to baby our tanks along. You can't cowboy tanks in this terrain, or you'll make a lot of extra work for yourself and the maintenance crew. Of course you should always be paying attention to your BoG [bowgunner] and tank commander too. You are only one of a crew, and in combat the big thing is teamwork— in your tank and in the unit. One thing that should always be checked before and after a mission is your track suspension. Your tracks have got to be tight at all times. In hot weather, air cleaners must be cleaned after each shoot because of dust.

'Ridgerunning'—M46 Pattons of 1st Marine Tank Bn. negotiate a ridge line as they move forward to engage enemy bunkers in January 1952. By this time experienced crews had moved the .50cal. M2HB Browning forward of the turret to allow both commander and loader to fire the heavy machine gun to the front with minimum exposure to enemy fire. Stowage space is augmented by fixing the dust shields in a vertical position. (USMC A159107)

'Mines are one of the big headaches of a tank driver. We have to be watching at every moment. Of course, some mines can't be seen. But there is one enemy trick I've noticed: sometimes the Reds have placed mines in the tracks where our tanks have gone before. I have found that when they do this, they just throw a little pile of dirt over the buried mine. If you're careful you can spot them and go around the area. We have had instances where the enemy buried a 50-gallon drum of TNT and then put a mine on top to set it off. One thing I'd like to see would be an escape hatch with a bigger lid on it, to keep it from being blown inside the tank. We use old drive sprockets welded to them now, as an expedient.'

Tanks in Defence

While tanks operated aggressively throughout the static phase of the war, they also proved invaluable in the defence. A typical action took place on the night of 21 September 1952 on Hills 854 and 812 in eastern Korea, when 'C' Co., 245th Tank Bn. was acting in support of a ROK division. Ten M46 Pattons were emplaced on the MLR with 'A' Co. and the remainder of 'C' Co. in reserve, ready to act should the need arise.

During the early hours of darkness both hills were subjected to heavy artillery fire, followed by a diversionary feint against Hill 812 and an attack by two enemy battalions on Hill 854. Throughout the night the tanks on Hill 812 sprayed each other with machine gun fire to clear the enemy who had infiltrated their positions. At daybreak the North

Koreans withdrew into nearby trenches, where they were pounded to destruction by tank fire.

Two tanks under the command of Master Sergeant Gregg were in a position to the south-west of Hill 854. They too came under artillery and mortar fire during the early evening of 21 September, followed by several infantry probes which were repulsed. This activity was followed by a further infantry assault, which forced the ROK defenders to withdraw. The tanks were ordered to stand fast, but radio contact was soon lost when their antennae were shot away. Fighting continued but, with the help of the few ROK soldiers remaining on the position, the tanks were able to hold their ground against repeated attacks which often raged within ten yards of the tank positions.

Hill 854 suffered the heaviest fighting of the

Surrounded by 90mm projectile fibre-cases, an M46 of 'C' Co., 6th Tank Bn., fires in support of 24th Infantry Div. at Song Sil-li on 10 January 1952. During the winter months some tanks were painted in a rudimentary camouflage scheme of broad, irregular white stripes over the base colour. Typical of Pattons in Korea, ammunition boxes and ration cartons are stowed along the fenders (trackguards) behind a simple wire frame. (US Army SC 389599)

battle. Squatting atop the primary enemy objective, the tanks dominated the surrounding terrain. The action began at 2030 on the 21st with a series of probes which were thrown back. At midnight an assault in company strength was met by the two tanks on the left flank of Hill 854, commanded by Lt. David Koch. Two crewmen were wounded and both tanks were forced to close down. Shrugging off heavy casualties, the enemy closed with the tanks and infiltrated their positions. North Korean troops crawled over them, smearing their vision blocks with mud and attempting to plug the main armament and machine guns. The Pattons fired on one another, traversing their turrets to knock the swarming enemy from the engine decks. The battle raged all night and by daylight the enemy had control of the hilltop as the defending infantry had been forced off the crest. Only the tanks remained.

The third tank on Hill 854, placed about 1,000 yards north of the others, was also in serious trouble. An enemy batallion had surrounded the area and radio contact had been lost. The narrow ledge on which it perched, weakened by heavy rains, began to crumble. The tank commander was ordered to withdraw to Lt. Koch's position but, seeing the area seething with North Koreans, he drove down to the bottom of the hill where 'A' Co. tanks were preparing to counter-attack.

Koch had observed this movement, and as his own position had become untenable he too decided to retire. Bumping the other tank as a signal, Koch descended the narrow trail, firing the while at the North Koreans nearby. The second Patton followed, but its clutch failed on the steep slope and it shuddered to a halt. At once, Koch's tank was hit by a bazooka shell and burst into flames which the fire extinguishers failed to quench. The crew abandoned the tank under a hail of bullets and scrambled down the hill to safety. The Patton stranded with the defective clutch was also struck by a bazooka round which penetrated the turret, killing the commander. A medical corpsman inside the turret opened the hatch but was instantly killed by small-arms fire. A number of grenades were lobbed into the open hatch—but the remaining crewmen managed to throw them out before they exploded, and secure it. A machine gun was now aimed through the puncture made by the bazooka, while inside a crewman attempted to hold a helmet over the

Most Commonwealth units in Korea employed the Universal Carrier in a variety of rôles. One of its principal tasks was the resupply of forward infantry companies, but in Korea it was often less than successful, and only found suitable for load-carrying over prepared roads. Its successor, the Oxford Carrier, was more effective over difficult terrain but, as they were few in number, many units employed the jeep and trailer for supply purposes. This Australian Pattern Carrier Mk. 2A illustrates the recognition sign adopted by several Commonwealth units—the Royal Air Force roundel. The version on the hull front is framed by a yellow square.

(Soldier)

hole. The gunner tried to escape through the belly hatch, but was knocked to the ground by North Koreans who dragged him in front of the tank and, in full view of his trapped comrades, bayoneted him and left him for dead. In spite of his wounds he crawled under the tank, where he remained unseen for several hours.

A counter-attack by ROK troops and 'A' Co. tanks now took place. The Pattons surged up the hills, jockeying abandoned tanks over the edge of the narrow track. By 1600 on the 22nd Hill 854 had been retaken. The aggressive employment of the tanks in the defence of the position and in the subsequent counter-attack proved to be a major factor in preventing a serious rupture of the front-line.

A Multi-National Army

In such a heterogeneous army as that of the UN forces in Korea there were often problems of communication. On one occasion a tank section of the 65th (Puerto Rican) Infantry Regt. was ordered to support Greek troops. None of the Puerto Rican tank crews could speak Greek and the Greeks could speak neither English nor Spanish. The orders, however, called for immediate co-ordinated action. The problem was solved by consulting the Korean boys who attached themselves to every UN unit. A boy who had learnt English from the Puerto Ricans was sent to discover whether any Koreans in the Greek

unit had learned to speak Greek. One was found. Orders were given in English to the Korean boy, who in turn gave them in Korean to the other boy. The second Korean then translated the orders into Greek. The operation was a complete success; but cases of failure in communications abounded and there were numerous variations on the theme 'Send reinforcements, we are going to advance' becoming 'Send three and fourpence we are going to a dance'.

Working in conjunction with South Korean troops presented particular problems as most of them had only a limited command of English. A conversation between a ROK officer, calling for US tank and artillery support, and an American liaison officer went as follows:

'Please, please, you must fire now. There are many, many Chinese in front of me now.'

'How many Chinese have you got?'

'There are many, many, MANY Chinese!'

Each time the Korean was asked for a precise estimate he simply added one more 'many'. Exasperated, the liaison officer demanded to speak to the unit American adviser.

'That goddam gook,' stormed the liaison officer, 'how many "chinks" you got there?'

To this came the reply: 'Hell, Captain—we got a goddam pisspot full!'

With a parting 'Why the hell couldn't that gook have said so?' the liaison officer ordered the tanks and artillery into action. (The word 'gook' was derived from the traditional Korean greeting 'Me gook' and at first was not the disparaging term for all Asiatics that it subsequently became.)

The brunt of the war was borne by the ROK Army which, while well-endowed with manpower, was woefully lacking in weapons and equipment. As indicated above, much of its support was provided by UN contingents. A few recollections by a troop commander from 1st Royal Tank Regiment give some insight into the hardships encountered by a typical South Korean unit:

'They had nothing. One went into the battalion command post, which was a very deep bunker. I first noticed that the maps were covered with a strange substance. Close examination revealed that they had been reduced to taking the French letters out of the American C-rations, carefully cutting them up and pinning them to the map to give an overlay surface. They were of course the rather crude French letters with chalk covering. They took Chinagraph surprisingly well.

'Another thing I noticed in the battalion command post were four men standing facing one of the walls with their hands in front of them. There was another man sitting on the ground, squatting Korean fashion, holding an ordinary field telephone. Suddenly, I noticed one of the standing men began to jump up and down. The man squatting got to his feet and walked across, took two wires out of the jumping man's hands which he connected to the field telephone and then carried on a conversation. I discovered that they had no telephone exchange whatsoever and only one telephone instrument in battalion HQ, so they had the four men holding wires who jumped on receiving a minor electric shock when the telephone was cranked at the other end. Once I saw utter chaos with all four men jumping together and I hurriedly left the command post.

During the static phase of the war there was no requirement for amphibious landings so the Marines employed their 'amtracs' in support of infantry. LVT(A)5s (Modified) of 1st Armored Amphibian Tractor Bn. are emptied of 75mm shell cases after an Independence Day shoot against Communist positions, on 4 July 1952. The LVT(A)5 (Modified) was a post-Second World War variant of the LVT(A)5, with a newly-designed bow to improve surfing characteristics, deletion of the hull machine gun, access doors in the hull sides and a fully enclosed turret. The vehicles are well entrenched behind a ridge line, with sandbags protecting their thin top armour from mortar fire, and hull access doors removed to allow easier escape and ammunition replenishment. (USMC A162962)

'One problem I had with the ROKs was that they were very fond of drinking petrol (I always wondered why the petrol level was going down so fast, which entailed problems of replenishment). They used to bring long bamboo tubes and put them down inside the tank filler caps at night and fill up their tins and get as high as kites on drinking your petrol. I finally observed one miscreant at it and went to the company commander and complained. He said show me the man and I'll have him shot. I said No, I don't think that is necessary. Then he said, Well, cut his hand off. I said No, I think that would be a pity. In the end they did catch one beggar and he was given a severe beating with spades and I had no more problems.

'While there was a language barrier, we overcame this by the use of a panorama sketch and numbering all the targets with Arabic numerals, which the Koreans could speak. They just sat on the back and shouted "Number One, Number One, Number One" and you would fire that target for them. I found that we had more first-aid kit on one Centurion than they had in the entire battalion. I began to discover what is meant by the term "walking wounded". They were normally brought to my tank however badly they were injured. We did what we could for them and then they had literally to walk to the MSR in the hope that someone would pick them up and take them to the dressing station.'

*   *   *

And so the war ground on, until an armistice was finally signed on 27 July 1953. Combat casualties were approximately two million on both sides and a further one million civilians lost their lives. Ever

Shermans of 'C' Sqn., Lord Strathcona's Horse, return from the frontline across the Imjin River. They were assigned to the 25th Canadian Inf. Bde. Group of 1st British Commonwealth Div.; 'B' replaced 'C' Sqn. of the regiment in Korean service from June 1952 to May 1953. Note placing of red/yellow arm-of-service flash and black unit code '41', white tank name, and yellow-on-red Canadian Forces in Korea insignia on the hull; see also Plate F2. Quantities of 76mm shells are carried in fibre cases in a cradle welded to the rear hull. (Canadian National Photography Collection SF-5156)

One of several technical innovations instituted by the Marine Corps during the Korean War was the tank-mounted searchlight, introduced in March 1952. Manufactured by the General Electric Company, the 18in. whitelight projector was employed to illuminate enemy activity in 'No Man's Land' and to counter massed infantry attacks at night. In one such action Marine tanks equipped with this device fought a night-long battle in support of the Turkish Bde. and inflicted numerous casualties, including more than 700 dead.

(USMC A164531)

since, there have been constant violations of the armistice agreement, averaging five a day, including 100 major armed provocations across the 155-mile truce line. Both sides have amassed powerful armoured forces along the 38th Parallel; and this far peninsula remains a constant threat to world peace.

The Plates

A1: T-34/85 of NKPA 109th Armoured Regiment, 105th Armoured Brigade; Seoul, 27 June 1950

Formed in October 1948, the 105th Armoured Bn. was the first armour unit of the NKPA. It was increased to regimental strength in May 1949, and by June 1950 had become the 105th Armoured Bde. with 6,000 men and 120 T-34/85s. The brigade had three tank regiments—the 107th, 109th and 203rd, each of 40 tanks—and a mechanised infantry regiment, the 206th. It also had an organic artillery batallion, the 308th, with sixteen SU-76 self-propelled guns. The 105th Armoured Bde. was raised to divisional status at the end of June 1950 following the capture of Seoul in conjunction with the NKPA 3rd and 4th Divisions. All three units received the honorary title 'Seoul Division'. In common with all North Korean tanks, the markings of this T-34/85 are limited to the vehicle number on the turret sides, an unusual addition being the slogan painted on a wooden plank across the glacis plate. It reads 'Annihilate the foreign invaders'—the *causus belli* invoked by the North Koreans for their invasion of the South. The ground colour of the vehicle is Soviet 'summer olive brown', very similar to US Olive Drab.

A South Korean armoured force was formed in April 1951 as part of the Infantry School near Kwangju. Equipped with M24 Chaffees and M36B2 Tank Destroyers, ROK tanks first entered combat in October 1951 on the east-central front. A South Korean M36B2 waits in support of 9th ROK Division as an assault begins on Hill 395, White Horse Mountain, north of Chorwon on 8 October 1952.

(US Army SC418366)

A2: M24 Chaffee of 24th Reconnaissance Company, 24th Infantry Division; Chonui, 10 July 1950

The first American tanks committed to battle in Korea were M24 Chaffees of this unit. In the unequal struggle against NKPA T-34/85s the Chaffees did not fare too well, but proved invaluable during the defence of the Pusan perimeter as dug-in self-propelled artillery. This particular M24, 'Rebel's Roost', is reputed to be the first US tank to see action during the war. On 10 July three M24s fought an action against a number of T-34/85s, losing two tanks but destroying one of the enemy. The markings on the front fenders— '24x', '24-R21'—indicate vehicle 21 of 24th Reconnaissance Co., 24th Infantry Division. The white stars on turret sides and glacis plate are obscured by mud.

B1: M26 of 1st Platoon, Company 'B', 1st Marine Tank Battalion, USMC; 'Battle of the Barricades', Seoul, 27 September 1950

The fire-position turret markings 'B11' in golden yellow denote the platoon leader's tank of 1st Platoon, Company 'B', 1st Marine Tank Battalion. White stars are displayed on turret sides, turret roof, glacis plate, rear decks and dust-shields. The detail view shows the rear hull marking; the USMC registration number and yellow diamond embarkation/movement symbol, with the figure '2' superimposed in black indicating second phase of landing.

An LVT3(C) attached to 1st Marine Engineer Bn. of 1st Marine Div. breaks up ice flows threatening the supports of Spoonbill bridge on 28 December 1952. The LVT3(C) was a post-war modification of the LVT3 with a machine gun turret, and aluminium hatches over the troop compartment, hence the suffix (C)—'Covered'. The Main Supply Route to several divisions in the front-line passed over these flimsy bridges and the vital task of keeping them in service made such improvisation necessary. When the rivers were in full spate the Communists often put tree trunks and demolition charges into the water upstream in order to smash bridge supports and sever supply lines. This was countered by employing tanks along the riverbanks to destroy dangerous debris with gunfire. (USMC A169702)

B2: M4A3 (76)W HVSS Sherman of 'C' Company, 72nd Tank Battalion, 2nd Infantry Division

This 'Easy Eight' displays the disruptive camouflage scheme of Earth Brown over the Olive Drab base colour adopted during the summer months. On the turret sides the tank carries a row of flags and unit insignia representing the UN contingents which the battalion had supported in action. From left to right—the United Nations flag; the insignia of 2nd 'Indianhead' Infantry Division; Turkey; 27th British Commonwealth Brigade; Netherlands; Republic of Korea, and France. The conventional front and rear hull markings are '2-72 △', 'C-22'.

C: M4A3(76)W HVSS Shermans serving in March–April 1951 with:
(C1) 89th Tank Bn.; (C2) 64th Tank Bn.; (C3) 'A' Co., 70th Tank Bn.; (C4) Tank Co., 65th Regimental Combat Team

In spring 1951 many American AFVs were bedecked with colour schemes representing ferocious tigers and dragons. The painting of such

designs during Operations 'Killer' and 'Ripper' was a ploy dreamed up by the Psychological Warfare Branch to instil terror in the Communists at the time of the Chinese lunar New Year, a festival of great significance in the Orient. Whether it did so is doubtful; but at least, in the words of a platoon commander of 89th Tank Bn., 'It puts us in the running with the Air Force boys with their painted 'plane noses!'

Each year in the Chinese calendar is symbolised by an animal; 1950 was the Year of the Tiger and 1952 the Year of the Dragon. (The omission, by design or default, of the logical use of the symbol for 1951 reminds us that at that time the Rabbit had a less than bellicose image—*Playboy* Magazine did not appear until 1953, so its 'bunny' had not yet become a symbol of masculinity, though it was to be emblazoned on many AFVs in a subsequent Asian war.) Few of these schemes outlasted the summer of 1951, and they did not reappear. A further choice example is illustrated as Plate H1 in Vanguard 26, *The Sherman Tank in US and Allied Service*.

C1: 21-in. star well forward on hull sides. Where USA-numbers were carried these were marked in 3-in white digits towards rear of hull sides (eg 'USA' above '30114745-S') and tank names were sometimes painted ahead or behind them, in white. Unit codes, eg '89△', 'C-16' on front and rear hull.

C2: Marking based on blue and white shoulder patch of parent 3rd US Inf. Div.; company unknown. Turret sides bore 15-in. '4' and 12-in. star; driver's name painted ahead of his station. Hull sides bore 15-in. 3rd Inf.Div. patch, without 'tiger', centrally; well forward, a 21-in. star; and between them, in two lines of 3-in. white capitals, 'Skeeter Hawk'.

C3: All additional markings seem, in the photograph used as a source, to be obscured by mud.

C4: Sherman of Lt. Williamson, commanding 2nd Pltn., with codes '3- 65-I', 'TK-21' high on the glacis. Starting above top point of 15-in. turret side stars was name 'Nelle' in approximately 3-in. white capitals. The 21-in. star and divisional patch were repeated on hull sides, but no other name or numbers are apparent. Note that this tank had a 3-in. white barrel band at the base of the gun, where it met the mantlet collar.

The quad .50s of an M16 of Battery 'A', 21st AAA AW Bn. (SP) fire on enemy positions in the vicinity of White Horse Ridge. Beside the driver's door is stencilled 'HELL'S FIRE', and below is the unit insignia of 25th Infantry Div.—an Hawaiian Taro leaf split by a lightning bolt. This gave rise to the M16's nickname within this unit of 'Quad-Lightning'.
(US Army SC 24346)

D1: Cromwell Mk VII Gunner OP of 45th Field Regt., Royal Artillery, attached to Reconnaissance Troop, 8th King's Royal Irish Hussars, 'Cooperforce'; at the Battle of Happy Valley, 3 January 1951

The Cromwells of 'Cooperforce' fought a desperate action at Chunghung Dong where, together with the Churchills of 'C' Sqn., 7 RTR, they covered the withdrawal of 29th Brigade to Seoul through an area known inappropriately as Happy Valley. 'Holy Smoke' carries the RA flash and the formation sign of 29th Brigade. 'FSO A 1756' (centre of hull front) is a shipping/movement instruction. The word 'None' across the turret front is a jibe directed at US 2nd Infantry Division which, wherever it went, displayed prominent signs stating 'Second to None'.

D2, 3: Daimler Dingo Mk2 W/T Scout Car, and Universal Carrier No. 1 Mk III, of 'C' Sqn., 8th King's Royal Irish Hussars; Battle of the Imjin River, 22–25 April 1951

'Harlequin', a Dingo of 'C' Sqn. HQ Troop, was commanded by Cornet John Venner, who was awarded the Military Cross for his gallantry during the battle of the Imjin River. 'Calypso Lady' was part of 'C' Sqn. Carrier Troop, which was commanded by Sgt. Rowan, who also fought with distinction, gaining the Military Medal. Both vehicles display the RAC arm-of-service

Flying a Turkish flag, an M46 of 1st Marine Tank Bn. perches on the skyline as it prepares to fire in support of the Turkish Bde., 25th Infantry Div. on 5 July 1953. Over the mantlet is a searchlight mounting-bracket and welded to the turret side a 'brass-saver' constructed from picket stakes. During the perennial ammunition shortages it was decreed that all brass projectile cases be retained and returned for re-use. On the rear fenders are jerrycans of engine oil—to the left 50W and to the right 10W. Both cans are inscribed '1st M.T.' and the vehicle number 'B14'. Beside the first-aid box on the rear hullplate is the tank/infantry telephone on which is written 'INF. PHONE USE IT!'   (USMC A173205)

sign with the unit serial '41' and the formation sign of 29th Brigade. Both vehicles were knocked out during the battle.

E1: M46 Patton of 'B' Co., 6th Tank Bn., 24th Infantry Division, 'Task Force Growden'; Munsan-Ni, March 1951
The 6th Tank Bn. carried some of the most impressive colour schemes on the 'Tiger' theme, complete with splayed claws, snarling mouth, staring eyes around the mantlet apertures and even whiskers below the gun. The number of this tank, painted centrally at the top of the glacis, is 'U.S.A.' over '30163007'; the unit codes at the bottom of the glacis are '8A-6△', 'B-19'.

E2: M4A3 Dozer Tank of HQ and Service Co., 3rd Engineer Bn. (Combat), 24th Infantry Division; March 1951
A variation of the 'Tiger' scheme displaying yellow stripes over the base Olive Drab. Markings follow the standard pattern, with those on the left (as viewed) indicating division and battalion ('24-3E') and those on the right company (HQ and Service) and vehicle number ('HS-102'). Note small name 'Nancy' below 'Hyzertiger II'.

F1: Centurion Mk 3 of 1 Tp., 'C' Sqn., 5th Royal Inniskilling Dragoon Guards, commanded by Sgt. James Bertrand'; Operation 'Jehu', 17 June 1952
By 1952 British tanks rarely carried Allied white stars, and markings are limited to the registration number 'O2ZR76', the arm-of-service sign and the insignia of 1st British Commonwealth Division. The vehicle name is 'Cavalry Charger', and on the turret bins is the squadron sign of a red circle shadowed in white. On the turret rear is a black callsign plate with '1A' inside a white circle denoting the Troop Sergeant's tank of 1 Troop 'C' Squadron. (For divisional insignia detail, see Vanguard 22, *The Centurion Tank in Battle*, Plate B.)

F2: M4A3 (76)W HVSS of 'C' Sqn., Lord Strathcona's Horse (Royal Canadians) (2nd Armd. Regt.), 25th Canadian Infantry Bde. Group, 1st Commonwealth Div.; Sami-chon, November, 1951

On arrival in Korea Lord Strathcona's Horse was equipped with M10 '17-pdr. SP Achilles IIC' Tank Destroyers, which were exchanged for M4A3E8 Shermans obtained from American stocks. Tank names began with the squadron letter, 'Calvados' being named after that delightful fiery Norman liquor. On the top left of the glacis plate is the insignia of Canadian Forces in Korea and on the right the arm-of-service sign with unit serial superimposed. These markings and the tank name are repeated on the rear hullplate. Typical of hilltop firing sites are the earthworks protecting the suspension, and the sandbags to the front saturated with sump oil to minimize dust-clouds when firing. Hung in the background is a Chinese propaganda poster. Such crude invective was often placed at night in front of Allied positions. Note that the American white star on the turret sides has been overpainted with Olive Drab, and the red circle sign of 'C' Sqn. has been substituted.

In the last month of the war the Communists staged numerous heavy attacks against the UN lines. One of the most ferocious battles took place at Pork Chop Hill, a company-sized outpost located forward of the 7th Infantry Div. Main Battle Positions. All logistical support had to be transported along a narrow track covered by enemy artillery and mortar fire. Due to constant shelling the road was only passable for tracked vehicles—maintenance of the road under fire was normally achieved by engineers dropping rock-filled sandbags from M39 Armoured Utility Vehicles. Being an open-topped vehicle, the M39 was vulnerable to mortar fire and shellbursts, so in the final weeks the newly arrived M75 Armored Personnel Carriers were used for supply tasks. In April 1953 the Armored Personnel Carrier Platoon (provisional) of M75s and M39s was organised. Throughout the final attacks against 'the Chop' (6–11 July 1953) the M75s struggled through the mud and shellfire, carrying ammunition and supplies to the beleaguered position, and returning along the rutted track with wounded and dead. During the battle more than 70,000 rounds of artillery and mortar fell on 'the Chop' and its single access road. Nicknamed the 'Lifesaver', the M75 was vital to the maintenance and eventual evacuation of the position. The photograph shows two M75s on 7 July 1953 at the waterlogged checkpoint area of 17th Infantry Regt., 7th Infantry Div., from where supplies and reinforcements moved forward to Pork Chop Hill. (US Army SC433163)

G1: M40 Gun Motor Carriage of 'C' Battery, 937th Field Artillery Bn., Eighth Army; April 1951

Each M40 within this battalion was given alliterative names beginning with the battery letter which embraced both words, e.g.

Angry **B**ulldog's **C**ourageous
Annie **B**ark **C**onfederate

In keeping with its name, this 'Long Tom' flies the flag of the Confederacy. Note unit codes '937F', 'C-21'.

G2: M41 Howitzer Motor Carriage of 'A' Battery, 92nd Armored Field Artillery Bn. (SP155); Pukhan River in support of 1st Marine Division, 24 April 1951

Known during the Second World War as the 'Gorilla', the M41 was based on the chassis of the M24 Chaffee. During the Korean War SP artillery pieces were called simply 'tanks'. This unit fought a distinguished action on 24 April 1951 when the battalion position was attacked by numerous Chinese infantry, killing 179 of the enemy at a cost of four dead and 11 wounded. The

92nd's nickname of 'Red Devils' is reflected in the device painted on hull sides, and was repeated on the sides of crewmen's helmets.

H1: M19 Gun Motor Carriage of 'B' Battery, 3rd Anti-aircraft Artillery Automatic Weapons Battalion (SP), 3rd Infantry Division; August 1952

Self-propelled anti-aircraft vehicles were used with considerable success in the ground rôle as close support for the infantry. M19s and M16s were frequently employed together to complement each other's characteristics: in the words of the 3rd AAA Bn. commander—'A few 40s on a bunker or machine gun emplacement will drive the enemy out, then we can mow them down with our quad-fifties.' Note vehicle code repeated on sign on sandbag emplacement.

H2: M16 Multiple Gun Motor Carriage of 'B' Battery, 15th Anti-aircraft Artillery Automatic Weapons Battalion (SP), 7th Infantry Division; Chae-jae, March 1951

Known variously as 'the grinder', 'meat-chopper' or more commonly 'quad-fifty', the M16 was an awesome weapon against exposed troops and even those sheltering in foxholes and bunkers. Such a weapon was also capable of prolonged saturation fire to 'box' infantry patrols in 'No Man's Land' as a counter to enemy ambushes. Side markings are an ornate 'Hell on Wheels' and a bee symbol, in yellow: codes are '7X-15AA', 'B10'.

H3: M15A1 Multiple Gun Motor Carriage of the Turkish Bde., attached to 25th Infantry Division; Hill 507 near Kumhwa, June 1951

Another SP AA weapon used in Korea was the M15A1 mounting a 37mm gun and twin .50cal. machine guns. 'Bozkurt', which means 'Greywolf', was a legendary animal of Turkish history; this vehicle was perhaps so named because the Turkish Brigade was fighting at the time beside the 27th Infantry Regiment—the 'Wolfhounds'—of 25th Infantry Division.

Notes sur les planches en couleur

A1 Cette brigade comportait 120 chars T-34, un régiment d'infanterie mécanisée et une unité de canons mobiles autonomes SU-76. Les chars étaient peints en vert olive russe avec des marquages simples sur la tourelle. La planche ajoutée à la caisse avant porte le slogan 'Écrasons les envahisseurs étrangers!'. **A2** On dit que le 'Rebel's Roost' ('Perchoir du Rebelle') fut le premier char américain opposé à l'armée nord-coréenne (ANPC). Marquages '24 X', '24-R 21' du char 21, 24th Recce Co., 24th Inf. Div.

B1 Le 'B 11' jaune indique le char du chef de peloton, 1er Peloton, Compagnie 'B'. Le '2' noir sur losange jaune est un code de débarquement, ici '2ème vague de débarquement'. **B2** Camouflage 'Earth Brown' et 'Olive Drab' d'été; la rangée de 'rubans' sur la tourelle indique les unités et la nationalité des contingents avec lesquelles ce char a servi.

C1, 2, 3, 4 Au printemps 1951, des têtes de 'dragons' ou de 'tigres' étaient peintes sur de nombreux chars américains d'après les symboles du calendrier chinois, apparemment pour faire peur aux ennemis superstitieux. Par manque de place, voyez les légendes plus détaillées dans le texte anglais.

D1 Ce char s'appelle 'Holy Smoke'; marquages rouges et bleus de la Royal Artillery et initiales 'RA'; c'était un char d'observation d'artillerie. Le cercle blanc sur carré noir indique la 29th Brigade anglaise. 'None' ('personne') sur la tourelle est une boutade vis-à-vis de la 2nd Infantry Division américaine, dont la devise était 'Second to None' (ici littéralement 'second de personne'). **D2, 3** Véhicules détruits au cours d'un combat acharné sur la rivière Imjin. Ils ont le marquage rouge et jaune du Royal Armoured Corps avec le code d'unité, et l'insigne de la 29th Brigade. Les deux chefs d'équipe furent décorés pour leur vaillance.

E1 Les codes d'unité signifient '8th US Army', '6th Tank Batallion', 'B Company', 'Char 19'. Une des peintures 'tigre' les plus impressionnantes. **E2** 'Hyzerstiger II' et 'Nancy' inscrits sur fond de peinture 'tigre', très visibles.

F1 L'étoile blanche était rare sur les chars anglais en 1952; les marquages se limitent au numéro d'immatriculation; code d'unité sur marquage rouge et jaune du Royal Armoured Corps; et insigne de la 1st Commonwealth Division. Le cercle rouge et blanc identifie le 'C Sqn.'. Il y a un 'l A' blanc cerclé de blanc sur une plaque noire à l'arrière de la tourelle pour indiquer 'Troop sergeant, 1 Troop'. **F2** Les noms des chars commençaient par la même initiale que celle de l'escadron. Ici, 'Calvados' appartient au 'C Sqn.'. Le marquage sur le bouclier est celui des 'Canadian Forces in Korea'. Propagande ennemie suspendue aux fils barbelés par les patrouilles de nuit ennemies.

G1 Codes d'unités '937 F' et 'C-21'. Les noms commencent avec l'initiale de la batterie. **G2** Notez l'insigne 'Red Devil' sur le côté de la caisse.

H1 Ces véhicules étaient utilisés en combat au sol pour défoncer les abris ennemis. **H2** Souvent utilisé avec les M19 pour anéantir les bunkers ennemis ('bunker-busting'). Appelé 'Hell on Wheels' ('L'enfer sur roues'); et note insigne abeille. **H3** 'Bozkurt' signifie 'loup gris', un animal turc légendaire.

Farbtafeln

A1: Diese Brigade hatte 120 T-34er Panzer, ein motorisiertes Infanterieregiment und eine Einheit von SU-76er Geschützen auf Selbstfahrlafetten. Die Panzer waren in sowjetischem olivgrün angemalt mit einfachen Turmnummermarkierungen. Des vorne am Rumpf angebrachte Brett trägt den Wahlspruch 'vernichtet die fremden Eindringlinge.' **A2:** Angeblich die ersten US Panzer, die gegen NKPA Streitkräfte kämpften, 'Rebel's Roost' (der Rebellenhorst) trägt Markierungen '24X', '24-R21' des 21. Panzers, 24th Recce Co., 24th Inf.Div.

B1: Das gelbe 'B11' bedeutet: der Panzer des Zugführers, 1. Zug, 'B' Kompanie. Die schwarze '2' auf der gelben Raute ist ein Landungscode, der die 'zweite Welle der Landungstruppen' anzeigt. **B2:** Die Tarnungsfarben Earth Brown und Olive Drab wurden während des Sommers benutzt; die Reihe der auf den Turm gemalten 'Bänder', zeigen die Einheiten und die nationalen Truppenkontingente, mit denen der Panzer gedient hat, an.

C1, 2, 3, 4: Viele US Panzer waren im Frühjahr 1951 mit 'Tiger' oder 'Drachen' -gesichtern bemalt, die Symbole des chinesischen Kalenders hervorrufen, angeblich ein Versuch, um abergläubische Feindestruppen zu beeindrucken. Aus Platzgründen werden die Leser für weitere Einzelheiten dieser Panzer an die einglischen Untertitel verwiesen.

D1: 'Holy Smoke' ist der Panzername; die rotblaue Markierung der Royal Artillery trägt die Initialen 'RA'—dies war ein Artillerie-Beobachtungspanzer; und der weisse Kreis auf dem schwarzen Quadrat ist das Zeichen der britischen 29th Brigade. 'None' auf dem Turm ist eine Spitzelei gegen die 2. US Inf.Div., deren Motto 'Second to none' (Niemandem nachstehend) war. **D2, 3:** Fahrzeuge, in schweren Kämpfen am Fluss Imjin zerstort. Beide tragen rotgelbe Royal Armoured Corps Markierungen mit der Codenummer der Einheit darübergelegt; und Zeichen der 29th Brigade. Beide Kommandeure wurden für Tapferkeit ausgezeichnet.

E1: Die Einheitscodes bedeuten: '8th US Army', '6th Tank Battalion', 'B Company', 'Tank 19'. Eines der eindrucksvollsten 'Tiger' Farbschemen. **E2:** Die Namen 'Hyzerstiger II', 'Nancy', sind über sehr auffälligem 'Tiger' Schema gemalt.

F1: Der weisse Stern wurde sehr selten von britischen Panzern bei 1952 gezeigt; Markierungen sind auf die Registrationsnummer begrenzt; Einheitscodenummer auf rotgelber RAC Markierung; und 1st Commonwealth Div. Abzeichen. Rot und weisser Kreis lässt das 'C' Sqn. erkennen; hinten am Turm würde ein weisses '1A' innerhalb eines weissen Kreises auf einer schwarzen Platte sein, welches den Troop Sergeant, 1. Troop erkennen lässt. **F2:** Die Namen der Panzer begannen mit dem Buchstaben des Schwadrons, dieser 'Calvados' gehort zum 'C' Sqn.; die Markierung auf der vorderen Panzerplatte ist die der Canadian Forces in Korea. Bemerke das Propagandaschild des Feindes, welches am Stacheldraht von feindlichen Nachtpatruillen aufgehängt wurde.

G1: Einheitscodes '937F', 'C-21'. Die Namen begannen mit dem Buchstaben der Batterie. **G2:** Bemerke das 'Roter Teufel' Abzeichen an der Rumpfseite.

H1: Diese Fahrzeuge wurden für Bodenkämpfe benutzt, zum Abbrechen von feindlichen Unterständen. **H2:** Oft benutzt in Verbindung mit M19, für 'bunker-busting'. Der Name ist 'Hell on Wheels' und bemerke das Bienenabzeichen. **H3:** 'Bozkurt' meint 'Grauer Wolf', ein legendäres türkisches Biest.

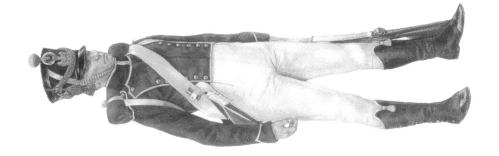

OSPREY
PUBLISHING

FIND OUT MORE ABOUT OSPREY

❑ Please send me a FREE trial issue
of Osprey Military Journal

❑ Please send me the latest listing of Osprey's publications

❑ I would like to subscribe to Osprey's e-mail newsletter

Title/rank

Name

Address

Postcode/zip   state/country

e-mail

Which book did this card come from?

❑ I am interested in military history

My preferred period of military history is _____

❑ I am interested in military aviation

My preferred period of military aviation is _____

I am interested in *(please tick all that apply)*

❑ general history   ❑ militaria   ❑ model making
❑ wargaming   ❑ re-enactment

Please send to:

USA & Canada: Osprey Direct USA, c/o Motorbooks
International, P.O. Box 1, 729 Prospect Avenue, Osceola,
WI 54020

UK, Europe and rest of world:
Osprey Direct UK, P.O. Box 140, Wellingborough, Northants,
NN8 2FA, United Kingdom

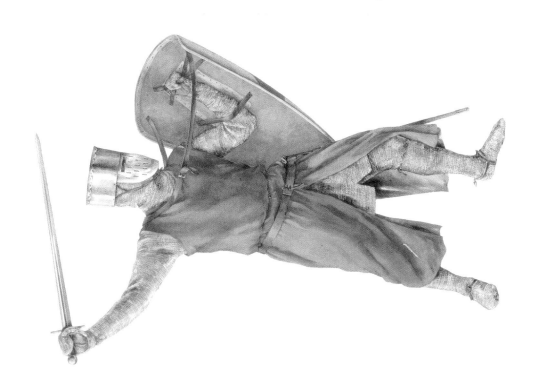

OSPREY
PUBLISHING

www.ospreypublishing.com

call our telephone hotline
for a free information pack

USA & Canada: 1-800-458-0454
UK, Europe and rest of world call:
+44 (0) 1933 443 863

Young Guardsman
Figure taken from *Warrior 22:*
Imperial Guardsman 1799–1815
Published by Osprey
Illustrated by Christa Hook

Knight, c.1190
Figure taken from *Warrior 1: Norman Knight 950 – 1204AD*
Published by Osprey
Illustrated by Christa Hook

POSTCARD